FIELDS OF DREAMS

FIRST PUBLISHED IN GREAT BRITAIN 2012
BY STEP BEACH PRESS LTD

28 OSBORNE VILLAS, HOVE, EAST SUSSEX BN3 2RE

WWW.STEPBEACHPRESS.CO.UK

A CIP CATALOGUE RECORD FOR THIS TITLE
IS AVAILABLE FROM THE BRITISH LIBRARY.

ISBN 978-1-908779-01-4

DESIGNED BY KATCH CREATIVE

PRINTED AND BOUND BY STAR STANDARD INDUSTRIES (PTE) LTD,
SINGAPORE

FRONT COVER PHOTOGRAPH: THE DELL, SOUTHAMPTON
(STUART CLARKE)

BACK COVER PHOTOGRAPH: THE GOLDSTONE GROUND, BRIGHTON
(STEWART WEIR)

HALF-TITLE PHOTOGRAPH: FILBERT STREET IN THE 1950S
(JOHN HUTCHINSON, OFFICIAL HISTORIAN OF LEICESTER CITY)

FIELDS OF DREAMS

GROUNDS THAT FOOTBALL FORGOT BUT THE FANS NEVER WILL

BY CHRIS ARNOT

In memory of my father, Ron Arnot, who introduced me to the joys,
frustrations and disappointments of supporting a football club.

ACKNOWLEDGEMENTS

MANY THANKS TO THE FOLLOWING PEOPLE FOR BEING SO GENEROUS WITH THEIR TIME, THEIR INFORMATION AND THEIR ANECDOTES, AND APOLOGIES TO ANYBODY THAT I HAVE INADVERTENTLY MISSED OUT:

IN NO PARTICULAR ORDER, TIM CARDER OF THE BRIGHTON AND HOVE COLLECTORS' AND HISTORIANS SOCIETY, IAN CHADBAND OF THE DAILY TELEGRAPH, DAVID MCKIE AND DAVID BRINDLE OF THE GUARDIAN, PETER PRESTON OF THE OBSERVER, MARK RADCLIFFE OF BBC RADIO, JOHN EDWARDS, GRAHAM EDWARDS, MARTIN MACKENZIE, LEIGH BOND, PATRICK FREESTONE, MARTIN KEMP, JOHN BALL, PETE KENDALL, BRUCE WALKER, DAVE LONG, STUART GARDNER, SAM MCNULTY, PHILIP WILD, JANE BARKER, KEN LOMAS, TIM HOLMES, PHIL DIXON, DAVID JENKINS, ADRIAN BUTTERS, BARRY MOSS, MIKE JONES, CHRIS SMITH, CHARMAIN DIBBEN, CLIFF LEE, SIMON MARLAND, STEVE BEST, HARRY TODD, LEN GRANT, EMMA TAYLOR, STEVE STEWART, BARBARA COWLING, RICHIE MORGAN, MARTIN JOHNSON, RON DAVIDSON, STUART BASSON, ANDREW JARVIS OF THE DERBYSHIRE TIMES, FRANK GRANDE, JOHN HUTCHINSON, JOHN WILLIAMS OF LEICESTER UNIVERSITY, DAVE STERNBERG, MARTIN BRODETSKY, BOB CHAUNDY, DAVE WATERMAN, ANDREW WATERMAN, BARRY AND CORINNE WHALE, PHILIP O'HALLORAN, DENNIS PAYTER, MIKE JAY, DAVE CROSSAN, KEN FOSTER, SHAUN CAMPBELL, DOUG EMBLETON, GEORGE BINNS, GWYN REES, RICHARD SHEPHERD, STEVE TUCKER, MIKE ULYATT, BRIAN TURNER, BERNARD LEVETT, TONY BLUFF, STEVE UTTLEY AND, LAST BUT NOT LEAST, POET AND RADIO PRESENTER IAN MCMILLAN.

PICTURE CREDITS

STUART CLARKE FRONT COVER, 12-13; JOHN HUTCHINSON (OFFICIAL HISTORIAN OF LEICESTER CITY), HALF TITLE PAGE, 73, 74-75; CENTRAL PRESS/GETTY IMAGES 9; BOB THOMAS/GETTY IMAGES 15, 45, 69, 71, 111; BARRY COOMBS/ EMPICS SPORT 19; TONY BLUFF 21; STEVE UTTLEY 23; SIMON GALLOWAY/EMPICS SPORT 25; GAIGER/GETTY IMAGES 27, 105; NEIL CROSS 28-29; PA/PA ARCHIVES/PRESS ASSOCIATION IMAGES 32-33, 63; THE BOLTON NEWS 35; PETER ROBINSON/EMPICS SPORT 39; PETE NORTON 41,43; CHRIS ARNOT 49, 54, 60-61, 67, 103, 108-109, 129 (TOP); MILLWALL FC 51, 55; MIKE JAY 57, 58; STEVE WOFFENDEN 66; ADAM DAVY/EMPICS SPORT 79; DAVID EDSAM (ALAMY) 81; TONY MARSHALL/EMPICS SPORT 84-85; STEWART WEIR 87, 117, BACK COVER; ANDREW HASSON 91; TOPICAL PRESS AGENCY/GETTY IMAGES 93; TONY MARSHALL/EMPICS SPORT 97; JASON TILLEY 99; NEAL SIMPSON/EMPICS SPORT 115; JOHN WALTON/EMPICS SPORT 120-121; KURT HUTTON/GETTY IMAGES 123; HUW EVANS AGENCY 127, 152-153; DAVID MCKNIGHT 129 (BOTTOM), 133; POPPERFOTO/GETTY IMAGES 135; PETER ROBINSON/EMPICS SPORT 139; RON DAVIDSON 140-141; HARRY SHEPHERD/GETTY IMAGES 143; ANDREW GALLON 146-147; GWYN REES 149; DOUGLAS MILLER/GETTY IMAGES 155; NEAL SIMPSON/EMPICS SPORT 159.

CONTENTS

INTRODUCTION

Football is big business. Everybody knows that. Football is also show business – increasingly so as the big clubs offer big money to lure big-time players from around the globe. Their presence sells seats at the Etihad and the Emirates, stunning stadia with sponsors' names and 21st-century facilities. But the loyalty of long-term fans was nurtured on crumbling terraces and in rickety stands that reared up from red-brick streets. They put up with discomfort, questionable safety standards, verbal and sometimes physical threats, watery Bovril and pungently primitive toilets.

Why?

For the camaraderie forged by a common cause; for the moments of magic that transformed a humdrum Saturday afternoon or a chilly, floodlit evening; for the unlikely victories against seemingly impregnable opponents; for the chance to say 'I was there.'

In the course of researching this book, I've travelled from the south coast to Wearside, from Swansea Bay to the Humber Estuary. I've met some wonderful people who've been generous with their time and only too happy to share their memories of Maine Road and Highbury, the Baseball Ground and the Goldstone Ground, the Dell and the Den, the Victoria Ground, the Vetch Field and many more.

They have met me at stations and conveyed me to the sites where their lifetime loyalties were forged; where they sang or shouted themselves hoarse or looked on in awe as the likes of Matthews, Shackleton, Best, Brady or Le Tissier performed fleeting feats of outrageous skill that are still talked about in pubs or clubs years later. Their fields of dreams are now buried under housing estates, supermarkets or car parks, or have simply been abandoned to let nature take its course. Sometimes there

might be a statue or a plaque roughly where the centre circle used to be. Soulless cul-de-sacs might be named after players who were part of local folklore at a time when they lived in the communities that paid to see them play rather than in remote mansions behind electronically controlled gates. And somewhere above the checkouts at Asda or Morrison's, there might be a display of photographs in glorious black and white of mufflered, flat-capped and gap-toothed men cheering wildly or waving rattles while players with brilliantined hair thumped heavy case balls into bulging nets.

Change was inevitable. As in so many other aspects of life, the 1980s saw to that. First the Bradford fire and then the Hillsborough disaster made safety legislation an imperative. The legal requirement for all-seater stadia meant that even the great cathedrals of football, such as Highbury or Roker Park, could no longer accommodate enough spectators to meet demand.

There are downsides to change, however. It's absurd that a small club such as Darlington was bequeathed a 25,000-seater stadium, miles out of town, named initially after the chairman and former safe-cracker who had it built. While health and safety laws have been rigorously applied, it seems, the authorities have not been quite so vigilant about the kind of people that are allowed to run football clubs.

'Darlo' fans are understandably nostalgic for the wasteland that was once Feethams, their characterful former ground – especially now that their new ground has been mothballed and they're having to play even further away at Bishop Auckland. There are supporters of other clubs, too, who yearn to be back in their old home. Coventry City's Ricoh Arena offers 32,609 very acceptable vantage points from which to watch football, but the move from Highfield Road has drained them of the resources to buy players remotely capable of filling those seats. The former ground was within walking distance of the city centre with plenty of pubs and places to grab a bite to eat on the way. It was there, well within living memory, that the club had its finest hours under Jimmy Hill in 1967 and John Sillett and George Curtis in 1987. What's more, the stands and the playing surface were in comparatively good nick compared with, say, Derby County's former home.

The Baseball Ground was cramped and outdated, summed up perhaps by the advert on the roof of the 'pop' side suggesting that the Bus Station café offered 'the best feed in town'. Derby's new stadium at Pride Park offers infinitely better facilities. But it was at the Baseball Ground that Clough senior produced sides that seemed to glide majestically over the mud. And it was at the Baseball Ground that Real Madrid were humiliated one memorable October night in 1975. No Rams fan among the throng that squeezed their way out of the gates and back on to those tight, terraced streets will ever forget the occasion.

Clough and Peter Taylor, his fellow deliverer of miracles to medium-sized clubs, are cast in bronze outside Pride Park, just across the car park from Starbucks. There are similar statues outside similar stadia on similar edge-of-town business or retail parks all over the country. Yes, the new grounds offer better views, better toilet facilities and marginally better catering. But football in those grounds is part of a package that might include conferencing facilities, party venues, executive restaurants, fitness centres, casinos, rugby league in parts of the north of England and rugby union in south Wales. And once a match is under way, no effort is spared to keep the crowd informed about the sponsors of everything from the players' shirts to the corner flags. It seems depressingly fitting that so many identikit stadia, usually sited

closer to motorway junctions than to city centres, are identified by corporate brands rather than local street names or landmarks. Even the exceptions, such as those at Arsenal, Brighton and Huddersfield, have grounds named after an airline, a credit card company and suppliers of healthcare. That's evidently the price that has to be paid to lavish ludicrous wages on pampered players, some of whom spend most of the season sitting on the bench.

All these changes have happened comparatively recently, over the past 20 to 25 years, while most clubs have their roots in the late 19th and early 20th centuries. There was a hell of a long time when not much changed at all. Now I'm not going to try to pretend that everything was better in 'the good old days', and quite a few of the contributors to this book undoubtedly feel far happier in their new surroundings. That doesn't mean, however, that they've forgotten where they came from.

Perhaps Simon Marland, club secretary and club historian at Bolton Wanderers, summed it up when I met him at the Reebok Stadium and he recalled the last game at Burnden Park in May 1997: 'Moving from there to here was like moving from a terraced house to a five-bedroomed detached. It's much grander, but you still remember the happy times in that terrace, even if it was falling down around you.'

I hope this book will bring back some happy memories for the many genuine fans out there who still feel the pull of their roots. Yes, there are Chelsea supporters in the Midlands and a hell of a lot of Manchester United followers in southern England, but for most of us, following a football club is a statement of local identity at a time when many a football club has become just another brand in a global economy.

AYRESOME PARK

Mark Cubitt has the sort of house that many Middlesbrough supporters would regard as possessing added value beyond the dreams of estate agents. On the face of it, the house is a 'compact' end-of-terrace in a modern development. But, to quote the mantra of those estate agents, location, location, location is everything.

A few feet from the front window stood the posts between which John Hendrie slotted home his and Boro's second goal against Luton Town on 30 April 1995. It turned out to be the winner. It also turned out to be the last goal scored at Ayresome Park, the club's home for just over a century.

Mark, now 39 and a civil servant, was in the nearby Holgate End at the time. 'Hendrie just controlled the ball in a crowded penalty area and found enough space to side-foot it home,' he recalls. 'It was one of countless goals that I saw here, many of them from Bernie Slaven.'

Now that goalmouth is in Mark's front garden, although he swears that is not the reason he bought the house. 'No, it's just a coincidence, but a pretty good one. Look out now and it's difficult to believe that this was once a football ground.'

That's true. Is there nothing to commemorate Ayresome Park? 'See that denim jacket?' he says, pointing to a grubby and crumpled garment draped over the fence dividing his front garden from a patch of public greenery. 'Try picking it up.' I do and I can't. The jacket appears to be made of solid brass and is welded to the metal of the fence. 'That marks one of the goal posts,' he assures me. So where's the other? 'Just there,' he adds, pointing to a small disc embedded in his drive. 'Over there is a brass jumper that marks one of the corner flags.'

Jumpers and jackets, of course, have been used by generations of kids to make rudimentary goal posts in public parks. So is that the idea?

'Something like that. It's very subtle.'

Subtle? I've never seen such an understated set of public sculptures. In the front lawn next door to Mark's is what looks like a large cow pat

NORTH KOREAN GOALKEEPER LI CHAN-MYONG FAILS TO STOP RUBEN MARCOS'S PENALTY DURING THE WORLD CUP FIRST ROUND MATCH BETWEEN CHILE AND NORTH KOREA AT AYRESOME PARK, MIDDLESBROUGH, 15TH JULY 1966. THE MATCH ENDED IN A DRAW AFTER NORTH KOREA SCORED IN THE 88TH MINUTE.

HARRY PEARSON

Author and columnist, writing in the *Guardian* about watching Boro'

'My formative football years were spent in the Bob End at Ayresome Park, surrounded by men brutalised in the chemical plants and fabricating sheds and leisure hours spent watching Dickie Rooks. It was not an environment that encouraged dolly mixtures, or jelly tots. Most of the men in the Bob End were gnarled combat veterans who favoured masculine sweets such as Paynes Army and Navy Drops . . . Once, aged eight or nine, on a freezing night on which the surrounding phalanx cackled in bitter glee at the sight of Huddersfield Town's youthful centre-forward Frank Worthington, whose long hair they took as a signal of the approach of Armageddon, I made the signal mistake of taking a sip of Oxo while I still had a Victory V lozenge in my mouth. It was the sort of juxtaposition of contrasting flavours that may inspire the radical TV food scientists, but even four decades later the recollection still makes me gag.'

Middlesbrough in the 1970s

pitted with football studs. Apparently that marks the spot where, on a July night in 1966, North Korea scored the goal that beat the mighty Italians 1–0 during the World Cup finals. And round the corner sits a pair of football boots on someone's front doorstep. That was the middle of the pitch. Around it are more discs coinciding with the old centre circle. They pass across a lawn and down a drive, disappearing at one point under a Suzuki Sports GS.

There are few people about. All we can hear are barking dogs and distant seagulls from the River Tees. It's difficult to believe that on Saturday afternoons the land on which this estate now stands once resounded to crowds roaring on the likes of Hendrie and Slaven, Bryan Robson and Gary Pallister, Bobby Murdoch and Alan Foggon, Wilf Mannion and George Hardwick. Not to mention a local lad, name of Brian Clough, who notched up 204 goals for the club in just 222 games.

There are statues to Mannion and Hardwick outside Boro's current stadium, the Riverside. Both joined the club before the Second World War, fought in the war and played for England after the war, alongside Matthews, Finney and Lawton. Murdoch and Foggon were members of the Boro side managed by Jack Charlton that romped away with the Division Two championship in 1974, anchored by a defence whose very names struck fear into visiting forwards: Platt, Craggs, Boam, Maddren and Spraggon.

'Craggs was aptly named,' says my guide for the day, Dave Crossan. 'But he also had class.' Murdoch was Different Class, according to the title of

his biography. 'He looked a bit like Benny the Ball from *Top Cat* by the time he came here,' Dave goes on, 'but he strolled around, found space and could put a ball anywhere he wanted.' And Foggon? 'He was a bit overweight as well, but the crowd loved him. They called him "the flying pig" because he had a habit of running straight at defenders as though they didn't exist. They'd either get out of the way or he'd flatten them. It worked in the Second Division, but not so well in the top flight.'

Dave is a former teacher, now a community worker, who drinks in my local. We've driven a hell of a long way this morning to look at his former home, No. 1 Addison Road, the side of which was once bang up against the back of the Holgate End. The Crossans lived here from 1952 until 1963 when he was 11 and the club bought the house from his parents. Aged four, he was once found trying to clamber out of the dugout by the players when they came in for training. 'Luckily, Ray Yeoman, who lived in our road, recognised me and took me home.'

The first thing Dave does when he gets out of the car is go looking for the telegraph pole that used to be just inside the ground and down which he shinned to get in to home games for 'nowt'. Back he comes a few seconds later to report: 'It's gone.' At least the landing window that he used to climb out of is still there. Just below the gable end, it's the only one on the expansive end wall of a house that must have been a little dark inside. 'It was. My dad had to get permission from the club to install the glass.'

Perhaps it never occurred to Middlesbrough officials that it would provide free access for a young rascal who should have been paying a tanner (six old pence, in case you're wondering) to stand in the 'Boys' Enclosure' at the Bob End of the ground. Some of his mates got in via the telegraph pole as well. 'I used to charge them thruppence,' he confides. (That's three old pence, or just over a penny in 'new' money.)

Didn't anybody catch you?

'They did eventually.'

So how did you get in after that?

'Over that high wall. It was a fence in those days and we jumped straight into a pile of grass cuttings left by the groundsman at the bottom of the steps behind the Holgate terrace.'

There are, of course, no steps and no terrace left. But there is one physical relic of the ground still standing. At the heart of what might be termed the new estate's village green is a whitewashed wall. 'That was part of the gents,' Dave assures me. 'There were two walls originally. One was for privacy, the other to piss up.'

We stroll on to the far end of the estate where the modern housing gives way to more traditional Victorian and Edwardian streets. On the main Ayresome Park Road, sharing a wall with a burglar alarm, is what's left of a large sign that looks vaguely familiar – and not just to Dave. In large red capitals it reads BOYS' EN . . . The CLOSURE part has evidently gone missing, I surmise, until it gradually dawns on me that I've been here before. In that Boys' Enclosure I mean. What's more, I paid for it with money I earned in 1959 when I was 10.

We were staying with my Auntie Elsie, who kept a Middlesbrough pub called The Broadway. Before opening time, I helped out by putting bottles on the shelves in bar, snug and smoke room for a woman called Mrs Catterick. On the Saturday morning she gave me a shilling and said to my uncle: 'Ee, he's a canny lad.' To which he replied, under his breath: 'Can 'e have another shilling?' That afternoon I went to Ayresome Park with the lad who lived across the road from the pub. Can't remember his name; nor can I remember much about the match, except that Cloughie was playing. And, yes, of course he scored. But this was still Division Two. There were two other prolific centre-forwards at the time and both were scoring for fun in the top flight. One was Bobby Smith of Spurs, the other Gerry Hitchens, my hero at Villa Park.

Having got these boyhood memories out of our system, Dave and I repair to the pub. No, not The Broadway but another big barn of a place called The Cleveland, which no doubt used to be packed out on match days. Sitting in splendid isolation in a side bar this Tuesday lunchtime is a former pupil of Dave's old grammar school, Ken Foster, who grew up in a similarly semi-cobbled street of blue sets on the other side of the ground. Ken went on to become a lecturer in sports law at Warwick University. Since retirement, however, he has moved back to the north and is now a season ticket holder at the Riverside.

He was first taken inside Ayresome Park on Boxing Day, 1949, when he was three. So he just happened to be part of the biggest crowd ever to cram in there: 53,596 for the visit of Newcastle United – and, needless to say, he doesn't remember anything about it. 'The first match I recall on the old ground was Bishop Auckland v Corinthian Casuals in an Amateur Cup replay in 1954. I remember being struck by how much the crowd got behind the Bishops, mainly made up of miners from the North East, against a bunch of southern public schoolboys.'

The crowd didn't always roar on the Boro with quite the same intensity, he recalls. 'When I first started going there, the players had to put in a big performance to win over the supporters. Funnily enough, the first time I ever felt there was an Ayresome roar was that World Cup game between North Korea and Italy. Although the place was half-empty, the crowd really got behind the Koreans. I think a lot of people saw

the effect of that and it dawned on them what might happen if they did the same for the Boro.'

The following season they found out. On 16 May 1967, Middlesbrough thumped Oxford United to gain promotion from the Third Division to the Second, roared on by a huge crowd. 'There were so many people clamouring to get on the pitch at full time that a wall collapsed,' says Dave. 'I remember my dad complaining about the number of "lasses" there. They weren't wearing the right clothes as far as he was concerned and they knew "nowt" about football.'

By now they're both in full reminiscence mode. Never mind Craggs, Spraggon and the rest of that legendary defence; the hardest Middlesbrough defender that Ken ever saw was Graeme Souness, who played at Ayresome Park from 1972 to 1978 before moving on

MIDDLESBROUGH'S AYRESOME PARK ABOUT TO RECEIVE THE ULTIMATE PENALTY:
CONVERSION TO A HOUSING ESTATE.

to Anfield. 'You could hear the crunch when he went into a tackle and you winced,' he shudders. He remembers the joy of his first floodlit game – a friendly against Sunderland in the 1956–57 season. 'Everything seemed so much more intense under lights. What's more it meant that you could read a book at night in our back yard.'

Far be it from me to interrupt the warm glow of nostalgia, but I feel impelled to steer the conversation round to the dark days of 1986 when the club suffered a financial crisis and came very close to going out of business. By that time they were back in the third flight and they had to borrow £30,000 from the Professional Footballers' Association to pay the players' wages. (Those were the days when 30 grand a week would pay for a whole squad rather than a single player.) At one point the gates of Ayresome Park were locked and the club kicked off the 1986–87 season with a 'home' game played at Hartlepool. With

10 minutes to go before the deadline for registering with the Football League, in stepped the current chairman, Steve Gibson, to lead a consortium that somehow raised the £350,000 required.

Gibson it was who, nearly 10 years later, led the move down to the Riverside. Those unchained gates from Ayresome Park were taken to the new ground as a symbol of the old. They're now on show outside the stadium, not far from the statues of Mannion and Hardwick.

Near where those gates once stood, meanwhile, metallic models of a denim jacket, a jumper and a pair of football boots are arrayed around a studded cow pat and the wall from what was once a urinal to signify that this otherwise unremarkable housing development was once a famous football ground.

THE BASEBALL GROUND

A glorious autumn morning and the sun is beaming down on the Strata Euphoria 'designer homes' development. The air rarely seemed so clear when this was the Baseball Ground, Derby County were at home and the foundry behind the 'pop' side was belching fumes. 'Every night match they carried out some process that involved releasing thick, acrid smoke that hung over the pitch,' recalls my guide, Philip Wild, who has on the back window of his car a sticker proclaiming him to be 'Derby and proud of it'.

Press photographers must have exhaled wheezy sighs of relief when new floodlighting was installed in 1972 to comply with UEFA specifications after Derby qualified for the European Cup. Meanwhile, the visiting giants of European football gulped with apprehension as they sniffed the air and heard the noise generated by a comparatively small crowd packed into stands and terraces and so close to the pitch that they threatened to burst an eardrum or two. As for the pitch itself, that must have propelled their hearts into their boots as their boots sank into the mud. How teams managed first by Brian Clough and Peter Taylor and, later, Dave Mackay produced such scintillating football on a surface like that is one of the tantalising mysteries of the game.

More used to the expansive Bernabeu Stadium, the players of Real Madrid could have been forgiven for feeling somewhat claustrophobic as they emerged from the tunnel in October 1975. They duly lost 4–1, largely thanks to a hat-trick from Charlie George, though they reasserted their authority by winning the second leg 5–1. Clough and Taylor would go on to deliver two European Cups to the Rams' bitter rivals, Nottingham Forest. Derby, however, never advanced beyond the semi-final. Still, the Real game was perhaps the most memorable of many vibrant European nights at the Baseball Ground. Philip was one of nearly 35,000 rammed in that evening at a time when the official capacity was around 33,000. 'I always stood on the pop side and, on this occasion, I'd come straight from work and brought my sandwiches and a flask of tea,' recalls the former social worker. 'I put the travel bag on the terrace in front of me but, come half time, there was simply no way I could bend over to pick it up.' That night he went home hungry but happy.

JOHN O'HARE OF DERBY COUNTY IN ACTION AGAINST STOKE CITY DURING THEIR DIVISION ONE
MATCH HELD AT THE BASEBALL GROUND, DERBY ON 11TH SEPTEMBER 1971. DERBY WON 4-0.

ADVERTISING SPACE WAS OFFERED ON THE ROOF OF THE POP SIDE. FOR YEARS IT PROCLAIMED THE QUALITY OF OFFILER'S ALES. AFTER THE BREWERY CLOSED, THERE APPEARED THE DUBIOUS ASSERTION THAT THE BUS STATION CAFÉ OFFERED 'THE BEST FEED IN TOWN'.

Looking at the goals again on YouTube, it's evident that the pitch was in better nick than usual for Real's visit. Well, it was comparatively early in the season. Apparently the surface was below street level – hence the poor drainage and the tendency for it to deteriorate as the season advanced. The Boxing Day match against Manchester United in 1970 produced an absorbing 4–4 draw on a surface reminiscent of Weston-super-Mare at low tide. But the pitch was even worse when Derby entertained the other Manchester team in April 1977. Archie Gemmill went down in the penalty area and the spot kick was duly awarded. Cue a lengthy search for the penalty spot, which appeared to have been buried under several inches of mud. City's goalkeeper, Joe Corrigan, offered to help by pacing 12 yards from the centre of his goal line, only to be booked for his cheek. Eventually the Derby groundsman, Bob Smith, was summoned on with a tape measure and a bucket of paint. Time passed. Players chatted. The crowd entertained itself. Then at last the referee blew his whistle and up stepped Gerry Daly to blast the ball past the unfortunate Corrigan.

Nearly 35 years on, a steel statue of three footballers on a plinth almost sparkles in the autumn sunshine, while the grass around it looks positively lush. Admittedly there's a discarded bottle of Stella Artois not too far from what might once have been that buried penalty spot and a clump of toadstools close to the former centre circle. 'There never was a mushroom in the Baseball Ground,' Philip mutters, as well he might. (It's the way he tells 'em.) Elsewhere there are saplings and fluttering flags emblazoned with the name of the developers. To the left we can see a

sports centre behind where the Osmaston End used to be. To the right, on the site of the former Normanton End, are the 'designer' homes of the newly aspiring inner-city dwellers – twee town houses with mock-Georgian front doors and Victorian-style street lamps in front of them. There's a Baseball Drive and a Keeper's Green.

And not far away are the familiar Victorian terraced streets that Philip trudged or cycled down from the age of 10 onwards. He's now 70, so we're talking about the early 1950s. 'The pavements were blue brick in those days and then, as now, the houses opened directly on to them,' he remembers. 'Residents used to open their front windows to sell sweets, cigarettes and programmes. Some installed rows of wooden rails in their back gardens and charged cyclists three old pence to leave their bikes.'

One of the roads was called Vulcan Street. It led directly to the Vulcan Works foundry, owned by Francis Ley, who laid out a sports ground for his employees in the 1880s. After visiting the United States in 1889, Sir Francis, as he was later dubbed, convinced himself that baseball was the coming thing. On this side of the Atlantic, however, it remained very much a minority sport. Admittedly Derby County won the English Cup at baseball in 1897, with one Steve Bloomer at second base. But Bloomer would go on to bloom, as it were, in the game that had really taken root on home soil. He scored both goals in a 2–0 victory over Sunderland in September 1895, as County eased their way into the ground, extended and developed by Ley, that would become their home

KEN LOMAS, 75
Lifelong Derby County fan and former chairman of Coventry Sports Trust

'The Osmaston Stand always was a pretty rickety affair. I remember standing in there during a high wind some time in the 70s when corrugated iron and bits of asbestos started to rain down on us. We spectators took evasive action and covered our heads, and I don't think anyone was hurt. Just as well. I can't remember who we were playing, but I do recall that the match carried on regardless.'

for the next 102 years. Bloomer banged in 317 goals in the English First Division, most of them for Derby, finishing second only to Jimmy Greaves as the division's all-time highest scorer. No wonder he remains a folk hero at the club.

There would be others. Perhaps the best-remembered Derby side in the pre-Clough era was the one that won the FA Cup in 1946. Among the stars were Raich Carter, Peter Doherty and Jackie Stamps, a battling centre-forward of the old school with a shot capable of bursting a leather football. 'I saw him play once towards the end of his career,' says Philip. 'All I remember is that he was a big bloke with no teeth.'

Another key member of that side was Walter Musson, better known as Chick, an uncompromising wing-half with a habit of depositing opposition wingers over the railings and into the terraces below. Stanley Matthews had to be particularly wary. Visiting teams would enquire nervously on arrival at the Baseball Ground: 'Is Chick playing today?'

Surprisingly, perhaps, part of the ground was almost empty as that 1946 side made their triumphant way towards Wembley. The Osmaston End had been damaged by a German air raid in January 1941, and remained out of commission. It wasn't entirely unoccupied, however, as some supporters were prepared to take a few risks. Having survived a world war, perhaps they weren't too worried about the threat of falling masonry or corrugated iron.

The capacity had increased to 38,000 in the years leading up to the war and would briefly expand again when Clough and Taylor brought champagne football to a brown ale stadium. A record crowd of 41,826 were bottlenecked in there for a match against Spurs in September 1969.

In June 1971, Jane Barker took an unusual phone call from Brian Clough. 'I'd just finished my A levels and was about to embark on a holiday job at Littlewoods before going to university,' the chemistry teacher turned schools administrator remembers. 'At the time we lived opposite the Cloughs and Brian had gone out for a Sunday night drink with my dad. I was just thinking about having an early night when Cloughie came on the line and said: "Jane, how much are Littlewoods paying you?" It was 10 quid a week. "Right. We'll pay you 12." The club telephonist had apparently walked out on the Friday afternoon. Trouble is that Brian hadn't told anyone else at the ground that he'd appointed me as her replacement. The club secretary Stuart Webb was somewhat irritated when I turned up at the dingy side entrance on the Monday morning and he discovered that I couldn't type and had no switchboard experience.'

Jane had to learn fast how to cope with the three incoming lines from the public and the one for ex-directory calls. 'The first time I answered that one, a voice growled: "Bill Shankly here."'

TIM HOLMES, 49
Graphic designer

'There never was much love lost between Derby and Leeds. One of my biggest memories of the Baseball Ground was the infamous punch-up between Francis Lee and Norman Hunter in 1977. The ref sent them off and they promptly started again, with Lee throwing the punches this time. The mood in the crowd turned from outrage to hilarity.'

PHILIP WILD, 70
Retired social worker

'I was driving near the ground on a weekday in the early 90s when I noticed the players getting out of a mini-bus with a net bag of footballs. One of them escaped and bounced across the road. We'd just bought Craig Short from Notts County for £2.5 million and he was the one who ran after it. I had to jam on the brakes. He looked up and waved an acknowledgement. I breathed a sigh of relief. We'd just paid a record fee for a player outside the top flight and I'd nearly run him over.'

'From Liverpool,' he added, somewhat unnecessarily. There would be other calls from the likes of Malcolm Allison and Frank O'Farrell before Jane heard an unexpectedly well-spoken voice on the ex-directory line. 'George Brown,' it said. 'I hadn't a clue who he was,' she recalls, 'until he sighed: "Remember Belper?"' Yes, it was that George Brown, MP for the Derbyshire constituency of that name and former deputy Prime Minister. She put him through to the would-be dictator of the Baseball Ground.

The players returned for pre-season training in July, passing to and fro through the office at regular intervals. 'They were really friendly,' Jane remembers warmly. A bit flirtatious? 'One or two now and again, but mostly they were family men with no side on them. Kevin Hector was a lovely bloke who went on to be my dad's postman once he left the game, and the flashiest car in the car park was Roy McFarland's Ford Capri. Cloughie drove a Rover 2000 in those days.'

Those unassuming players would go on to deliver Derby's first League title the following year, while Clough would manage Brighton briefly and Leeds even more briefly before transforming Forest. His fall-out with Derby chairman Sam Longson has been well documented elsewhere. Suffice it to say that although Cloughie left the Baseball Ground in 1973, he never left the hearts of devastated fans. Dave Mackay would deliver another League championship in 1975 and

Derby would have their moments in subsequent decades. But the heady days of the early and mid-70s would never return.

All the same, there remains a big demand for football in a one-club town with passionate support. The all-seater requirement that followed the Hillsborough disaster left the ground with a capacity of not much more than 18,000. Proposals to extend the Baseball Ground came to nothing and the decision to move finally came to fruition in 1997. Alas, Derby lost the final match at their old ground 3–1 to Arsenal in May of that year.

Pride Park, sited across the road from a Land Rover dealership on a business park, is everything the Baseball Ground was not – spacious, with modern facilities and even a built-in Starbucks. Across the car park is a handsome bronze of Clough and Taylor, albeit splattered by disrespectful pigeons. The surrounding plaza of black and white marble is inset here and there with circular milestones marking the distance to other significant stadia. So we learn that Wembley is 121 miles away, the San Siro, Milan, 700 miles and the City Ground, Nottingham, 13 miles. Via Brian Clough Way, it might have added. The Baseball Ground, we're told, is just one mile. Or rather it was. The current reality is Baseball Drive and Keeper's Green on the Strata Euphoria designer homes development. The ground itself lives on only in the myriad memories of diehard Rams fans.

FANS ON THE TERRACES SAY GOODBYE FOR THE LAST TIME. 11TH MAY 1997.

THE BASEBALL GROUND | 19

BELLE VUE

'Belle Vue' is an expression used more often in the Dordogne than Doncaster. Quite how the French phrase for a beautiful view came to be applied to Doncaster Rovers' former ground is a mystery. Certainly the *vue* is not too *belle* from up here on a muddy bank where I'm standing with club historian Tony Bluff.

What was once one of the biggest and best-kept pitches in the land is now a wasteland of waist-high grass. 'This is the first time I've been back since we left six years ago and it's pretty devastating to see it in the state it is,' Tony admits.

With building work apparently due to start towards the end of 2012, nature in the meantime is rapidly reasserting itself. Brambles are spreading. Saplings stand on the brink of tree-hood. Not only here on the bank behind the old Popular Side, but also on what's left of the terraces and stands.

Over the years poor old Belle Vue has suffered from neglect, mining subsidence, an arson attack and, more recently, an explosion. An attempt to burn down the Main Stand in June 1995 caused extensive damage. Nine months later the club chairman at the time, Ken Richardson, was arrested after an evening match against Fulham. A four-year prison sentence followed on the grounds that he had paid a former SAS soldier to commit arson as a means of claiming money from the insurance company.

'It was the lowest point for the club,' Tony recalls, 'except that we were still in the League at the time. The following season was our first in the Conference and we were struggling to avoid relegation to an even lower level. By the end of the 1998–99 season we'd just about survived, but crowds were down to the 1,000 mark.'

From then on the only way was up. Incoming chairman John Ryan invested heavily in the club and Rovers returned to the Football League in 2003. Five years later 'Donny' had reached the dizzy heights of the Championship. In the meantime, the club had moved from the Earth Stadium, as Belle Vue briefly became known after a sponsorship deal with a Rotherham-based finance company, to the Keepmoat Stadium, sponsored by a building firm and predictably sited near yet another of those edge-of-town retail parks.

VERSUS LUTON TOWN DECEMBER 1953. MCMORRAN AND HARRISON FOILED BY KEEPER STRETEN.

IT IS MID-JULY, 1997. IT IS HOT.

BARNSLEY ARE IN THE PREMIER LEAGUE,

AND IN MY HEAD OUR SEASON

IS LAID OUT AS SIMPLE AS AN UNDERGROUND MAP

OR A CHILD'S DRAWING OF THE SOLAR SYSTEM.

MID-JULY, A PRE-SEASON FRIENDLY

AGAINST DONCASTER...

The opening lines of 'Home Support' by Ian McMillan, performance poet, broadcaster and bard of Barnsley,
distinctly underwhelmed by the prospect of visiting Belle Vue before Old Trafford, Anfield and the Emirates

Belle Vue, as we shall continue to call it, had been quietly laid to rest when nearby residents were woken by a thunderous explosion in the early hours of 7 February 2007. Two men had apparently broken into the Main Stand and one flicked open his cigarette lighter. Not a good idea when a previous intruder had nicked the boiler and left the gas pipes exposed. The two men were conveyed to hospital and, in one case, to a specialist burns unit. Meanwhile, part of the Bawtree Road had to be closed for two hours while scattered debris was collected.

Five years on we can see the traffic flowing freely beyond the ruins of that much-abused Main Stand. Tony, now 75, saw his first game here in 1955. So how does he feel looking out over his former field of dreams?

'I did miss it when we first moved out and I probably still do. The capacity was down to around 10,000 at the end because so many parts of the ground had to be closed for safety reasons. The Keepmoat has already hosted a full house of 15,001 against Leeds – not sure who was the one – but it's like so many others. Lego grounds, I call 'em. Belle Vue was a throwback. You felt that you knew what it was like to watch football in 1910.'

Ironically in the circumstances, it wasn't built until 1922. Charles E Sutcliffe, president of the Football League at the time, came to open it and hailed it as one of the best grounds in the North. Five years later, the main stand at Rovers' former ground in Bennetthorpe was jacked up and moved here on rollers. It became the Family Stand, surviving until 1985 when its wooden structure was deemed unsafe in the wake of the Bradford City fire.

Other parts of the ground, notably the Town End terrace, were boarded up as time went on. Steve Uttley, who now works at the Keepmoat as head of media and communications, remembers coming to the old ground as a Sheffield Wednesday supporter in the 1970s and watching a match from the Rossington End through a fine film of dust. 'There was all this loose gravel on the terracing giving off clouds of it, which meant we could hardly see the far side of the pitch,' he says. 'It was a bit different from Hillsborough.'

And very different from the Emirates Stadium, from which Arsenal departed for a long trip up the M1 to play a Carling Cup quarter-final here in 2006. 'They were gobsmacked by the state of the place,' says

DERELICT STAND

Tony with some relish. 'Only one shower worked and that was issuing cold water. It was December as well.' What happened on the pitch? Well, Doncaster achieved a very creditable 2–2 draw. But the Gunners won the penalty shoot-out and headed south, presumably praying that they would never have to visit such a tip again. Barnsley, who had more idea what to expect, had taken the precaution of turning up for a match the previous season already changed, thereby avoiding the horrors of the away dressing room. They'd have a shower when they got home, thank you very much.

For some supporters the move to the Keepmoat must have seemed like a blessed relief, even though the club was relegated back to the third flight in May 2012. For others Belle Vue will always harbour fond memories. 'The match that everybody of my generation talks about was in 1950–51 in the old Division Two,' says Tony. 'Manchester City were promoted that year, but we beat them 4–3 in front of a crowd of well over 30,000. It was a bit before I started coming here,' he adds wistfully.

He was a Belle Vue veteran of two years' standing, however, when Doncaster's Harry Gregg became the most expensive goalkeeper in

the world. In 1957 he signed for Matt Busby's Manchester United for a staggering fee of £23,000. During the previous year Busby had cast a judicious eye over Tony's all-time favourite Donny player, Alick Jeffrey. He was 17 at the time, a precocious inside forward who had already been heralded as a genius by no less a figure than Stanley Matthews. Jackie Milburn had been impressed, too, having seen this strapping son of a colliery blacksmith make his debut for Doncaster aged 15 years and 229 days. 'He would have complemented another big strong lad, Duncan Edwards, in the United team,' Tony goes on. 'It was a pity that neither would showcase their talents at the top beyond their very early years.'

We all know what happened to Edwards. But how was Jeffrey's career cut short?

'He broke his leg playing for England under-23s in October 1956. Eventually he did get back in the Rovers side in 1963, after the insurance angle had been sorted out. And he scored a lot of goals, albeit at a lower level.'

BILLY BREMNER HAD TWO SPELLS AS MANAGER AT BELLE VUE. HE LED DONCASTER TO PROMOTION TO THE THIRD DIVISION IN 1981 AND BACK DOWN AGAIN TWO YEARS LATER. THE FOLLOWING YEAR HE TOOK THEM UP ONCE MORE. IN EMERGENCIES HE WOULD SOMETIMES PLAY HIMSELF. INDEED, HE WAS STILL OCCASIONALLY TURNING OUT FOR THE RESERVES IN HIS LATE FORTIES. IT WAS UNDER AN UNDERSTANDABLY TIRING BREMNER THAT BELLE VUE'S EXTREMELY LARGE PITCH WAS SHORTENED BY EIGHT YARDS.

Back in the mid-1950s, it seems, smart Alick had been a hit on and off the field. He played the guitar in the dressing room to provide backing for a singer by the name of Charlie Williams. Eventually that singer would become famous far beyond the boundaries of Doncaster by telling jokes on a politically incorrect 1970s show called *The Comedians*. For now, though, he was Doncaster's centre-half and the first black player whom fans of Rovers and many other clubs had come across. No doubt he suffered his fair share of abuse from away supporters, but it was Charlie's way to make jokes about it. He also made jokes about his footballing ability, maintaining that he couldn't play himself but he could 'stop them as could'.

To Tony's mind, he did himself a disservice. 'I liked to watch him,' he says. 'He was very enthusiastic and fit and never let his opponents get to him because one tackle from him would soon make them keep their distance. As we say in Yorkshire, he was a "muck and nettles" player.'

'Muck and nettles' seems a rather apt description of what remains of Belle Vue 90 years after it was hailed by the president of the Football League as 'one of the best grounds in the North'.

FANS DURING THE LAST EVER MATCH AT BELLE VUE. 23RD DECEMBER 2006.

BOOTHFERRY PARK

There aren't too many hills in Hull. The city and the surrounding fields form by far the flattest landscape in all Yorkshire. Even Bunker's Hill was man-made – a steep terrace at one end of Boothferry Park that eventually became the double-decker South Stand with seating for 2,500 'upstairs'.

'I always preferred to stand,' says Mike Ulyatt, former advertising manager at the *Hull Daily Mail.* 'The terraces were where the banter was, and if you didn't like the surrounding company you could always move. I wouldn't buy a season ticket now because I might be stuck next to the biggest bore in the world.'

Mike saw his first match here in 1948 when he was nine and the ground itself was just two years old. It had originally been planned in 1929; work finally started in 1932 but financial setbacks and, eventually, the Second World War intervened. The site was used by the Home Guard and, later, as a tank repair depot. It was hardly surprising then that the playing area was not as good as first envisaged when it finally hosted Hull City's opening match here against Lincoln. 'The drainage improved when they dug it up and laid a layer of rotten fish on top of cinders,' Mike assures me. 'It became a very good pitch.'

You'd think it might smell a bit, but as Mike explains, 'There was plenty of soil on top. Mind you, there was always a whiff of fish in those days if the wind was in the right direction.'

Trawling is one of many traditional trades in the north of England to be devastated over the past 30 years or so. But the docks here would have been bustling with activity and brimming with fish when Hull City AFC was founded back in 1904. After a spell sharing with one of the local rugby league teams, they moved to nearby Anlaby Road, close to The Circle cricket ground where Yorkshire sides used to play at least once a season until the 1990s. The Circle is now buried under the KC Stadium, home of Hull City since Boothferry Park closed in 2002. After nearly a century, it could be argued, the football club had gone back to its roots. And, once again, it's sharing with the Hull FC rugby league side.

Back at Boothferry Park, meanwhile, preparation for house-building work has finally begun after the leases expired on two supermarkets

24TH MARCH 1930: HULL FOOTBALL CLUB CAPTAIN, M BELL, LEADS HIS TEAM OUT ONTO THE PITCH.

HULL CITY CROWD, PROBABLY EARLY 1930s VERSUS MIDDLESBROUGH. THE ANLABY ROAD END.

HULL CITY HAD SPECIAL DISPENSATION AT ONE TIME TO PLAY MATCHES ON CHRISTMAS DAY AS WELL AS BOXING DAY IN THE ERA WHEN THE DOCKS WERE OVERFLOWING WITH FISH AND THE CITY'S TRAWLERMEN WERE AWAY FROM HOME FOR MUCH OF THE YEAR. CROWDS WERE SIZEABLE, OVER 45,000 TURNING OUT FOR A GAME AGAINST ROTHERHAM IN THE 1950s. KICK-OFF WAS EARLIER THAN USUAL, BUT THERE WOULD INEVITABLY BE TRIPS TO THE PUB AFTER THE GAME FOR A SEASONAL PINT OR THREE. RESULT: HUSBANDS AND SONS WERE RARELY HOME MUCH BEFORE THE QUEEN'S SPEECH. HULL'S LONG-SUFFERING HOUSEWIVES WERE TOO OFTEN LEFT WITH DRIED-UP TURKEYS AND SPROUTS THAT WERE EVEN MORE OVERCOOKED THAN IS CUSTOMARY.

that stayed on site long after the football crowds had left. Kwik Save and Iceland were invited to embed themselves into the stadium's structure when the club was undergoing grave financial problems in the 1990s.

Mechanical diggers are pecking over what remains of Bunker's Hill. It's now almost as flat as the rest of Hull. A fading sign above a fence topped by barbed wire proclaims HOME SUPPORTERS ONLY, and below it Strata Homes are promising 'A collection of luxury two, three and four-bedroom homes'. Mike has already written to the developers asking if some of the roads can be named after well-known players of the past.

There could be a Carter Close, perhaps. Or perhaps not. There is, apparently, a road in Hull already named after the great Raich Carter, who came to the City in 1948 as player-manager and led them to the Division Three North title soon afterwards. Surely, though, there should be a Wagstaff Way. After all, Ken Wagstaff was voted by fans the greatest Hull player of all time during the club's centenary celebrations in 2004. Wagstaff played 378 times for the Tigers between 1964 and 1975, scoring 173 goals, many of them in partnership with Chris Chilton, who scored even more. There might be a Davidson Drive after Andy Davidson, the right-back who made more appearances at Boothferry Park than anyone else, between 1952 and 1968. And we could go on to name roads after more recent Hull heroes – Dean Windass, perhaps, a local boy whose goal in the play-offs took Hull to the Premier League for the first time in 2008, and another two-term stalwart, Keith Edwards, who scored against the then-mighty Liverpool in a cup tie in 1989 before the Tigers went down valiantly by three goals to two.

Might there even be a Houghton Highway to celebrate left-half Ken Houghton, part of the vibrant Hull side of the mid-1960s? Mike recollects that he had a 'superb game' against Forest in an FA Cup fourth-round tie in February 1966. 'Can't remember him making a mistake.' he says. 'The Tigers won 2–0 with Terry Heath scoring both goals and there were over 38,000 in Boothferry Park.'

Nearly 47,000 were there in February 1954, when Spurs made the long trek to Hull and back for a fifth-round tie. 'My dad had a large ship's bell and I borrowed it for the game,' Mike confides. 'A guy behind us must have got fed up with me ringing it because he took it off me and said he'd give it back at the end of the match.' And he was as good as his word, cheered no doubt by the Tigers' last-minute equaliser. Mike still relishes describing how it happened.

'I can see this vividly today, even after 58 years. City's Danish international Viggo Jensen came down the left wing on the East Stand side of the ground and had just got into their penalty area when Alf Ramsey obstructed him and the referee gave an unlikely penalty. Viggo duly scored and Eddie Bailey was booked for protesting, an unusual thing in those days. Mind you, Spurs won the replay 2–0.'

The biggest crowd ever turned up in February 1949. Over 55,000 were sardined into Boothferry Park to see City lose 1–0 to Manchester United. Mike wasn't one of them, although his dad was. 'He'd queued all day to get a ticket the weekend before, but because he was only a little bloke, he couldn't see a thing. He came home at half time.'

He was lucky to be able to get out. Bryan Turner was eight at the time and one of many children allowed to sit on planks resting on bricks laid out on the cinder track around the pitch. 'We got there at 11.30 with our lunches in knapsacks,' he recalls. Kick-off was at three and there was no chance of getting back through the crowds to use the toilets.'

So what did they do?

UNLIKE THE KC STADIUM, BOOTHFERRY PARK NEVER HOSTED TOP-FLIGHT FOOTBALL FOR HULL CITY, BUT IT DID STAGE A MATCH IN THE OLD FIRST DIVISION BACK IN AUGUST 1971. A CROWD OF 25,099 TURNED UP TO SEE LEEDS UNITED DRAW 1–1 WITH TOTTENHAM. AT THE TIME, LEEDS WERE BARRED FROM ELLAND ROAD AS PUNISHMENT FOR CROWD TROUBLE AT A HOME GAME AGAINST WEST BROM.

FLOODLIGHTS WERE SWITCHED ON AT BOOTHFERRY PARK FOR THE FIRST TIME IN 1964 FOR A MATCH AGAINST BARNSLEY. THE TIGERS EVIDENTLY ADAPTED TO EVENING FOOTBALL MORE QUICKLY THAN THEIR VISITORS, WINNING 7–0.

'Bottled it, I suppose. I really can't remember. What I do remember was that my hero, the Hull goalie Billy Bly, played on with a broken arm. There were no substitutes in those days.'

Later in life, Bryan would become a bank manager in Sheffield. Bernard Levett, who was also sitting on a pitch-side plank that day, would become the man who sold the tickets from Hull's central Paragon Station to and from Boothferry Halt, where anything up to 12 packed trains would disgorge supporters on match days. Bernard would always be on the last train in either direction. 'We were allowed to watch three-quarters of the game before we had to go off into a little hut and issue tickets for the return journey,' he remembers. 'If it was a gripping game, we'd hold on until the last minute and then make a run for it. Sometimes you'd hear a roar and you knew the Tigers had scored. You'd groan inwardly at having missed it, but you couldn't really complain because you'd got in for free. And you had to be quick issuing the tickets because the last train left 20 minutes after the end of the match. So you'd bag up the money, scurry up the slope and jump in the guard's van.'

Mercifully, he was never robbed or seriously assaulted. 'You'd sometimes get a bit of trouble on the trains, particularly when Manchester United fans came here in the 70s. And some Sunderland supporters once started rocking the ticket hut to and fro with me inside it. You just had to grin and bear it.'

Neither Bernard, Bryan nor Mike were among the 14,162 who turned up for the very last game at Boothferry Park in December 2002. The Tigers, alas, gave them no cause to roar. They managed to lose 1–0 to Darlington, despite the away side playing with 10 men for most of the second half. Six years later Hull would be promoted to football's top flight for the first time in their history. But for now the supporters streaming away from the old ground for the last time felt a bit like the city and the surrounding countryside – a bit flat.

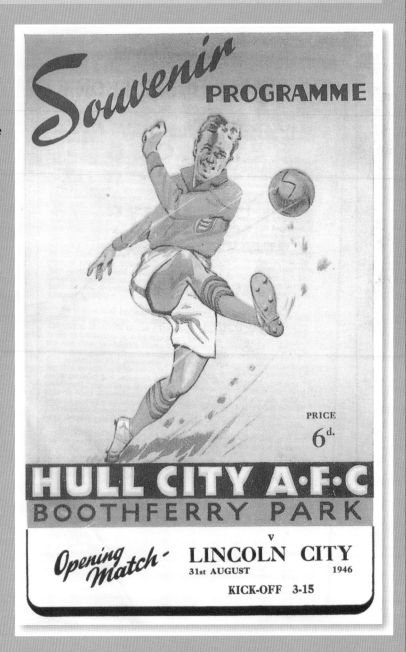

Souvenir PROGRAMME

PRICE 6d.

HULL CITY A·F·C
BOOTHFERRY PARK

Opening Match - LINCOLN CITY
31st AUGUST 1946
KICK-OFF 3-15

HULL CITY SUPPORTERS STAGE A GOOD-NATURED PITCH INVASION TO MARK THE END OF THEIR TEAM'S LAST EVER MATCH AT THE BOOTHFERRY PARK GROUND, AFTER THEIR NATIONWIDE LEAGUE DIVISION THREE MATCH AGAINST VISITORS DARLINGTON. 14TH DECEMBER 2002.

BURNDEN PARK

You'd have to be getting on a bit to remember the Burnden Park disaster. It preceded the carnage of Hillsborough by 43 years. Thirty-three people were crushed to death in Bolton that day, some of them having only recently returned to these shores after fighting in a world war. Another 400 or so were injured.

The date was 9 March 1946, and kick-off was approaching for the second leg of a sixth-round cup tie against Stoke City when they closed the gates. It wasn't just that a place in the semi-final beckoned. There was also the not inconsiderable drawing power of Stoke's Stanley Matthews. This at a time, remember, when crowds were up all over the country as football fans revelled in the return of their beloved game in the first full season after the war.

The turnstiles had ceased turning at 2.40 with a capacity crowd, officially given as 65,419, wedged inside. Bolton Wanderers had attracted bigger crowds before the war – nigh-on 70,000, indeed, in the 1933–34 season. On this occasion, however, the Burnden Stand had not yet reopened after being requisitioned by the Ministry of Supply.

Cliff Lee was 15 at the time and one of over 28,000 already uncomfortably close to one another at the end known as the Railway Embankment. He was behind the goal but comparatively high up as he looked on with mounting concern. 'A high wooden fence on the Manchester Road side was broken down and thousands more surged in,' he recalls. 'In front of me the crowd began to sway, moving sideways like a wave. After a while I could see children being passed over heads. Then it was grown men. Bodies were being laid out on the pitch.'

By this time, the referee had ordered the players back down the tunnel. Cliff takes up the story again: 'Eventually they emerged and played out a meaningless 0–0 draw. I think the officials were worried about what might happen had they simply abandoned the match. When it was over, the crowd behind me broke down another fence at the back of the embankment and we got out by trooping over the railway line. Back on the street, I could see men staggering along, stripped to the waist and bleeding in some cases. Their clothes had simply been torn off their backs. Jackets and shirts hung in tatters around their trousers. And when I finally made it back to our street, women were standing outside their houses, waiting to see if their husbands would come home. The news had been on the wireless and spread like wildfire.'

SAM ALLARDYCE SUMS UP THE AGONY OF BOLTON WANDERERS 1—0 HOME DEFEAT BY
EVERTON IN THE SECOND LEG OF THE LEAGUE CUP SEMI-FINAL ON FEBRUARY 16 1977.

'I wish they'd never moved from Burnden Park. If you were in town during the day, you could decide there and then to go to a match. Now you have to plan in advance and get a train all the way out to Horwich. And the atmosphere's not so good since we lost the Burnden Terrace. I used to stand there with my dad, who first took me to the ground when I was six. John McGinlay and Owen Coyle were my heroes. Coyle wasn't as successful as a manager, but that's not necessarily his fault. The Premier League is all about who's got the most money.'

Those women were probably better informed than the players. Matthews later recollected the events of that dreadful day as follows: 'In our dressing room again we heard more rumours about the increasing number of casualties. Yet it was not until I was motoring home that evening that the shadows of the grim disaster descended on me like a storm cloud.'

An inquiry was set up under Justice R Moelwyn Hughes. Something must be done to restrict crowds, it concluded, or it would happen again. In the end, nothing much was done, and it did happen again. Not at Bolton, but at Ibrox Stadium, Glasgow, in 1971 when 66 were killed and, of course, at Hillsborough in 1989 where the death toll was 96. After Hillsborough something was done and Lord Taylor's prescription changed football for ever. Bolton was just one club that eventually moved to a brand new ground as a consequence of his report.

The Reebok Stadium seems a long distance from Burnden Park, and not just in terms of what it represents. 'We're six miles away,' I'm told by club historian and, indeed, club secretary Simon Marland shortly after my train has finally come to rest at Horwich Parkway. This is not just edge-of-town; it's beyond the town borders and on the margins of open country. With a vicious wind whipping down from bleak and brooding Lancashire moorland, it's a relief to be shown into Simon's office, just off the swish and spacious reception area that is the gateway to

various executive suites and the home of a plaque commemorating a visit by Sir John Major in April 1997, when the Reebok was brand new. Major was Prime Minister at the time, but not for much longer. His government was on the way out as Bolton were on the way up.

They were already winners of the Championship when they played their last game at Burnden Park in May of that year. Final score: Bolton Wanderers 4, Charlton Athletic 1. Simon will never forget it. 'There were grown men crying that night. Moving from there to here was like moving from a terraced house to a five-bedroomed detached. It's much grander, but you still remember the happy times in that terrace, even if it was falling down around you. Football's like life insofar as there are peaks as well as troughs, and it's important that you savour the peaks. My lad was 12 and a ball boy at the time. "Before we leave," I told him, "I want you to come with me and stand on the Burnden Terrace." He's 26 now and he can remember it like yesterday. A night game at Burnden with everybody singing was something special.'

Simon is 52 and an accountant by trade. 'My first love has always been football not finance, but these days the two are more and more intertwined,' he says in a telling reflection on the times. Above all he is a supporter. He's missed only one game, home or away, since 1975. 'That was because I was involved in an accident on the way to Watford in 1981,' he says, almost apologetically.

BURNDEN PARK PROVIDED THE BACKDROP TO LS LOWRY'S PAINTING *GOING TO THE MATCH*. THE ORIGINAL WAS BOUGHT BY THE PROFESSIONAL FOOTBALLERS' ASSOCIATION FOR £1.9 MILLION IN 1999. THE GROUND HAS FEATURED ON CELLULOID AS WELL AS CANVAS; PART OF AN ARTHUR ASKEY FILM, *THE LOVE MATCH*, WAS SHOT AT BURNDEN PARK IN THE EARLY 1950S. IN 1962, THE RAILWAY EMBANKMENT MADE AN APPEARANCE IN *A KIND OF LOVING*, STARRING ALAN BATES AND JUNE RITCHIE.

He was brought up within a mile of Burnden Park and spent much of his school holidays on the forecourt, booting balls against its outer walls. 'Every now and then we'd sneak in only to hear "Gerrout, you little boogers" from Harry Nuttall, who was a general dogsbody by that time. He'd been full-back in the 1923 side that won the first FA Cup Final to be played at Wembley. What I'd give now to be able to sit down and talk to him.'

Not much chance of that. Nuttall died in 1969. But since then Simon has interviewed many another old player, including his former next-door neighbour but one, George Hunt. 'He was one of the few people round there who didn't give us a bollocking for playing football in the street,' he recalls. 'He came to Bolton after playing for Tottenham, Arsenal and, briefly, for England. Because he worked on munitions, he carried on playing here during the war and for a short while after. Then he came back on the coaching staff in 1948 and was still here when we won the Cup 10 years later. As a centre-forward of the old school, Nat Lofthouse always said he was his mentor.'

Ah, yes, Lofthouse, the Lion of Vienna and the toast of Bolton. 'Every club has an icon,' Simon says. 'We just happen to have two.'

Who was the other one?

'Joe Smith had a similar goal-scoring record. Between 1908 and 1926 he scored 277 goals in 492 games. Nat got 285 in 503 between 1946 and '61. He stayed on to become coach, then manager, left for a short period in the 70s and then returned as executive club manager. He lived all his life in Bolton. Salt of the earth he was and hard as nails – a bit like Tommy Banks, who was left-back in that '58 final. I showed Tommy round the Reebok one day and we went into the dressing rooms. "What are those?" he asked suspiciously. And when I told him, he said: "foocking hairdryers! Doost not have towels?" You could see what these blokes would have been like playing football. Jimmy Greaves hated coming to Bolton. "If Roy Hartle, the right-back, didn't get you," he said, "Tommy Banks would. And he'd deposit you into the cinder track around the pitch."'

It could be argued that there is another Bolton legend of more recent vintage. Like the late Duncan Edwards, Sam Allardyce was a son of Dudley; like Edwards, he looked like a grown man when he was still in his teens and could have played in any position. Comparisons end there. Big Sam settled on centre-half, and was part of the team that won promotion from the old Division Two in 1978. But it was after the club had left Burnden Park that he became manager for an eventful eight years, including a top-six finish in 2004–05. 'In his first season he took us to the play-offs and two cup semi-finals,' says Simon before adding ruefully: 'We lost the lot.'

'Before the war, they used to sell hot black puddings from barrows on the way to the ground. Sometimes they'd be wrapped in paper and sometimes served between two slices of bread. No knives and forks were provided so don't ask me how you were supposed to slice open the casing. One day a match was called off for some reason. The crowd didn't turn up, but the barrows did. It became known locally as Black Pudding Saturday because the sellers ended up giving the puddings away to passers-by.'

Bolton lost Allardyce in 2007. After spells at Newcastle and Blackburn Rovers, in May 2012 he took West Ham up to the Premier League, passing Bolton on the way down. But he still keeps a house in the town where, one suspects, his heart lies and where he made his name. And what of the ground where he first made it? Well, the writing was on the wall for Burnden Park when the club sold off part of the Railway Embankment to Normid, a subsidiary of the Co-op. It meant that away fans had to be squeezed in next to a supermarket. There's a revealing picture in one of Simon's books on Bolton of John McGinlay turning away in triumph after scoring against Liverpool in an FA Cup third-round tie in 1993. Over 21,500 were inside Burnden Park that day, but no spectators are visible in the background. Instead there's a brick wall.

The site is now owned by Asda and, judging by its size, it takes up much more than a corner of the old railway end. At least the Burnden Park Pie Shop is still standing across the Manchester Road – a little outpost of local distinctiveness surrounded by soulless warehousing that could be anywhere in post-industrial Britain. And at least Asda has made some concession to local sensibilities by putting on display a series of historic Bolton Wanderers photographs high on the wall opposite a line of checkouts that seems to go on and on. And on.

There's a picture of Jimmy Seddon lifting the FA Cup aloft in 1929. It was his – and Bolton's – third triumph at Wembley in six years. And here's Lofthouse doing the same in 1958, alongside manager Bill Ridding. Next to it is a shot of Lofthouse scoring his second goal that day by barging Manchester United goalkeeper and Munich hero Harry Gregg into the net. To get a better view, I go behind the checkout and stand with my back to an Asda special offer on giant packs of cheese-flavoured Quavers with the calorie count prominently displayed.

Food manufacturers are obliged to provide that sort of information in minute detail. Our society is much more conscious of health and safety than it was just after the war, a time of real austerity when football was cherished as one of the few entertainments that could be afforded by the working man. Among the otherwise celebratory photos high on the opposite wall is one of a sea of flat caps on the Railway Embankment that once stood where shoppers are currently browsing the aisles and filling their baskets while being serenaded by bland background music.

The picture was taken by the chief photographer of the local paper on 9 March 1946, and I don't have to tell you what happened next. For all the seductive appeal of nostalgia, there are times when you have to accept that in football, as in life, some things do get better.

VIEW OF BOLTON WANDERERS FANS ON THE TERRACES AT BURNDEN PARK FOR THE TEAM'S
FINAL MATCH THERE BEFORE THEIR MOVE TO THE REEBOK STADIUM. 25TH APRIL 1997.

THE COUNTY GROUND

There was a time when most regional newspapers had a Saturday evening football special. It was usually known as the 'pink 'un', the 'blue 'un' or even the 'green 'un', depending on the colour of the paper. The Football Post in Nottingham went for plain white, but some of the readers were tickled pink one evening in the 1970s when a headline read: 'Stags held by Cobblers'.

The Stags were Mansfield Town. And the Cobblers? Northampton Town, of course. Northampton was once famous for making shoes rather than mending them, but only a pedant would expect football supporters to call themselves the Cordwainers. What seems more likely is that, until quite recently, the Cobblers were never short of locally made boots. Now theirs are probably made in China like everyone else's.

The term 'cobblers' was no doubt regularly uttered by Northampton's long-suffering fans in 2011–12 to describe the quality of football they were enduring at Sixfields, their home since 1994, until a revival in the second half of the season hauled them to safety. For a while they had been propping up the fourth tier and eviction from the Football League loomed. Not for the first time. That 1993–94 season was evidently traumatic. Having moved grounds when the season was already under way, the Cobblers finished bottom of the pile and only escaped the dreaded drop when it was deemed that Kidderminster Harriers' then undeveloped Aggborough stadium was not fit for the Football League.

Had Northampton still been resident at their old home, it might have been a close call between them and Harriers as to which could claim the least suitable arena. The County Ground was never designed to host football. It was essentially a cricket ground, owned by Northamptonshire County Cricket Club. Still is. 'The land was donated to Northants by a local benefactor under the condition that they had to allow other sports in there,' Town's historian Frank Grande explains. 'But cricket always had the upper hand. The football club had to spend money doing up stands that were never theirs.'

Not too much money, mind you. One side of the ground was completely open, rather like Sheffield United's Bramall Lane in the days when Yorkshire CCC were regular summer visitors. In Northampton's case, however, it was the football club that eventually felt obliged to move. By that time they had been tenants for the best part of a century, having played their first game here in 1897.

FANS PACK INTO THE COUNTY GROUND VERSUS FULHAM, 1966. THE LARGEST EVER CROWD OF JUST
OVER 24,000 WATCHED AS NORTHAMPTON LOST 2–4 AND WERE RELEGATED FROM DIVISION I.

'I was in that record crowd against Fulham and also here when we had the lowest attendance of 942 against Chester City [in 1985]. But the game I'll never forget was beating Leeds 2–1 in 1966. George Hudson nutmegged Jack Charlton and went on to score on his debut. Hudson didn't want to come here, but he'd fallen out with Jimmy Hill at Coventry. Coventry fans didn't want him to come here either. Some of them were so disgusted that they used to travel down to watch him play. Thanks to them, there were over 21,500 in the ground that day – nearly 7,000 more than the previous home gate against Newcastle.'

DAVE BOWEN EXPERIENCED THE HIGHS AND LOWS WHILE MANAGING NORTHAMPTON. FIVE YEARS AFTER LEADING THEM TO THE DIZZY HEIGHTS OF THE FIRST DIVISION, HE WAS BACK IN CHARGE AT THE COUNTY GROUND WHEN MANCHESTER UNITED CAME TO TOWN FOR A FIFTH-ROUND FA CUP TIE. UNITED WON 8–2, SIX OF THEIR GOALS COMING FROM GEORGE BEST.

Frank started watching the Cobblers in the 1950s when he was seven or eight. He's 63 now and works nights in the postal sorting office. But he's found time to write five books on his beloved club, including one on a boyhood hero. Tommy Fowler joined Northampton in 1945, having played alongside Tommy Lawton and Joe Mercer at Everton before the war. He stayed for 16 seasons. His position as an old-fashioned outside left meant that Frank had a particularly close view of Fowler's feet. 'When I was a kid, I used to sit on the front of the duckboards that used to be laid down in the gap where the football pitch ended and the cricket boundary began. The adults stood up, so you had to jump up sharpish if we scored in case someone fell on you. Health and safety wouldn't stand for it these days. And there was a five-foot drop at the back of those boards.' When the ball was booted over the boards and onto the cricket field, ball boys were stationed to try to cut it off before it reached the square, which was usually roped off.

The shortcomings of the County Ground as a place to watch football were graphically described by long-term fan and local sports reporter Mark Beesley in his book *Champagne Cobblers*. No, the title is not ironic. It focuses on the 1986–87 season when Northampton romped to the Division Four title. That was also the season when the Main Stand had to be closed for safety reasons. As a result, the media found themselves covering a match against Port Vale from the cricket press box, 200 yards from the action.

Mark recalls: 'Armed with a pair of antiquated binoculars, which I believed had last seen service during Montgomery's campaign against Rommel at El Alamein, I settled down for an afternoon of surreal entertainment.' Surrealism evolved into farce four minutes from the end when the Cobblers brought the score back to 2–2 after a goalmouth scramble. It was mid-December and the County Ground floodlights were not the brightest. 'Eight or so confused and flagging football writers and broadcasters, with deadlines looming, turned to one another in various bewildering states,' writes Mark, who eventually had to climb down three flights of stairs and walk all the way to the Hotel End to ask spectators who had scored. The general consensus was that it was Phil Chard, who was duly credited by the media. No one has argued since. Certainly not Chard.

As the lines between the cricket and football seasons became increasingly blurred, there were times when relations between the groundsharing clubs became strained. 'In the early 70s we were drawn away to Crewe in the first round of the League Cup,' says Frank. 'We held them to a draw but the replay also had to be played in Crewe because the cricket club wouldn't allow us to use the County Ground. And during the cricket season, they used our pitch as a car park. One player who came here for transfer talks asked why there were black marks in the penalty area. He was told: "That's the oil from the ice cream van."'

PHIL ROBINSON VERSUS MANSFIELD 11TH OCTOBER 1994 DURING THE LAST EVER MATCH AT THE COUNTY GROUND.

Ultimately, though, it wasn't relations between the winter and summer game that brought about the parting of the ways. It was the dilapidated state of the football ground. The cost of replacing the old wooden Main Stand to meet new safety demands in the wake of the Bradford City fire was particularly daunting. 'They pulled it down and replaced it with what the fans called the "Meccano Stand", which was really scaffolding poles with seats in.' Frank pauses for a moment to get his bearings and reckons we're standing roughly where the stand straddled the halfway line.

Today we're looking out over the always vaguely cheering sight of a totally enclosed cricket ground – a promise of summers to come. The pitch has been moved a few yards since the Cobblers upped sticks and such is the immaculate state of the outfield that it's difficult to imagine the grass on this site once being pitted by studs or skidmarked by sliding tackles on wet Saturday afternoons. It's difficult, too, to conceive of the din kicked up by home fans in the Hotel End, with its low roof acting as an echo chamber.

Supporters were particularly voluble during the 1965–66 season when they briefly basked in the sunlit uplands of the old Division One. Yes, Northampton Town were in the top flight! No wonder Frank regards Dave Bowen as his all-time favourite Cobbler. The former Arsenal and Wales wing-half started his career at Northampton and returned as player-manager in 1959 before guiding the club from the Fourth to the First Division in five seasons.

It couldn't last, and it didn't. When they lost to 4–2 to Fulham on 23 April 1966, in front of a record crowd of 24,523, the Cobblers set off on an even quicker journey in the other direction. They remain the only club to go from Fourth Division to First and back again in nine seasons.

And still they don't own their ground. Sixfields is rented from the borough council on a 125-year lease. Its position, out on the edge of town with the usual suspects – a KFC, a drive-thru' McDonald's, Bella Pasta and a multi-screen cinema – seems somehow symbolic. On the way here we've passed Franklin's Gardens, home of the town's much more successful rugby club. 'They get five-figure crowds while we struggle to get 5,000,' Frank gloomily points out.

Poor old Northampton Town FC, seemingly doomed to stay in the shadow of cricket and rugby. They didn't even manage to win their last fixture at the County Ground, going down 1–0 to Mansfield of all sides. On that occasion the Stags just couldn't be held by the Cobblers.

THE DELL

The moment came in the 89th minute. The score was Southampton 2, Arsenal 2; the date, 19 May 2001. The occasion: the last competitive game at The Dell. The club was preparing to move to St Mary's Stadium, close to its roots as the St Mary's C of E Young Men's Association, founded in 1885. The referee was looking at his watch as Dave Waterman turned to his son Andrew and said: 'Do you think we still have a magic moment left to come?'

They did. 'Immediately Matt Le Tissier brought that ball out of the... well, out of the universe and spun. Bang. Top corner. Once we'd calmed down, I turned to Andrew again and said: "That was absolutely ridiculous."'

If God sided with a team nicknamed the Saints, he could hardly have answered supporters' prayers more miraculously. Le Tissier had played his entire career at The Dell and was, according to Dave, 'the greatest player ever to turn out for the club'.

That's quite a claim when you think about the competition. From Shilton to Shearer, Southampton could put out a hell of a team of players who've graced the ground over the past 45 years or so. Admittedly they'd be heavy in the attacking department, with

Kevin Keegan and Mick Channon – he of the whirling-arm goal celebration – Peter Osgood and Frank Worthington, to name but four. Then there was Ron Davies, who scored 12 goals in 10 consecutive games in his first season for the club. Oh, yes, and Danny Wallace. Didn't his brothers play here as well?

'They did,' Dave confirms. 'Rod and Ray were twins. Danny scored one of the best goals I've ever seen. Goal of the season it was voted. It was an overhead scissor kick against Liverpool. We beat them 2–0 here, but they still pipped us to the title that year. It was our highest ever finish.' And it came under Lawrie McMenemy, the man who always came over on the telly as a genial Geordie. Eight years previously he'd led the Saints to an FA Cup Final victory over Manchester United.

A HANDSHAKE BETWEEN KEVIN KEEGAN OF SOUTHAMPTON AND TOTTENHAM HOTSPUR GOALKEEPER RAY CLEMENCE (RIGHT) AFTER
THEIR FIRST DIVISION MATCH AT THE DELL IN SOUTHAMPTON, 31ST OCTOBER 1981. KEEGAN AND CLEMENCE WERE FORMER
TEAM-MATES AT LIVERPOOL, AND CONTINUED TO PLAY FOR ENGLAND TOGETHER. TOTTENHAM HOTSPUR WON THIS MATCH 1–0.

CHARMAIN DIBBEN, 32
Bookseller

'My dad took me to the Dell when I was about five. The first thing I noticed was all the names carved into the back of the wooden seats in front of us. He found a space and carved mine in with a key. Christian name only, mind you. There wouldn't have been room for our surname: Mavriodakis.'

TONY GARDNER, 65
Builder

'I used to live just off Archers Road, very close to the Dell, back in the 1960s. There was a little pub – the Gateway I think it was called – that was like being in someone's front room. On match days you were standing shoulder to shoulder in there, which was good preparation for being in such an intimate ground. If you were at the front, you felt you could have reached out to tap the linesman on the shoulder. And there were times when the players seemed to be right up against you, particularly when there were corners and throw-ins. You could hear the banter between the players, including some effing and blinding.'

As far as we can see, however, there is no McMenemy Court here in the courtyard of the block of yellow stone flats built where The Dell once stood. There's a Le Tissier Court, of course, a Wallace Court, a Channon Court and a Stokes Court – the latter after Bobby Stokes, who scored the winner in that Wembley final. And there's a Bates Court after the late Ted Bates, otherwise known as 'Mr Southampton', former player, manager, director and president of the club, who also has a statue to himself outside St Mary's.

There may be a McMenemy Mansions or a Lawrie Lane round here somewhere. If so, we've missed it. There is, though, a sign saying 'No Ball Games' – an ironic postscript for an area that housed not only The Dell but also Northlands Road, headquarters of Hampshire County Cricket Club until 2001 when they, too, moved to a more expansive home.

And there's a Crossley Place. Crossley? Dave is temporarily flummoxed by that one. Then it dawns on him. 'That might be Mark Crossley, the former Forest goalie and the only man to save a Le Tiss penalty.'

Well, well, well: a generous gesture to be sure. It certainly wouldn't have happened had Crossley played for Portsmouth. Alan Ball had two spells here, as a player in the 1970s and manager in the 1990s, and he admitted to being surprised by the hostility between the two clubs. 'I've been involved in three other local derbies – the Merseyside and North London derbies as a player and in Manchester as a manager – and the feeling here is as high as anywhere,' he wrote in the foreword of *Saints v Pompey: A History of Unrelenting Rivalry* by Dave Juson.

Dave Waterman, on the other hand, is one of those who don't regard supporters of other teams – even near neighbours – as aliens from another planet. He's 58, a freelance quantity surveyor, and a Saints season-ticket holder who follows them home and away. But he was brought up in Fareham, borderline country between the two ports, and admits that there was a time when he used to go to The Dell one week and Fratton Park, Portsmouth, the next. He now lives in Horndean, close to the brewery that once produced Gale's ales, and very much Pompey territory. 'I'm a rare animal round there,' he confides after driving 18 miles from the family home to the scene of his greatest footballing memories.

'Two remarkable performances stick in the mind from my occasional visits to The Dell. Both came from the visitors. One was from George Best who scored four goals for Manchester United before half-time. He was then taken off because it was deemed that he'd done enough. The score remained 4–0. The other was from Ruud Gullit when he was player-manager at Chelsea in the late 90s. Southampton were winning 2–0 when he brought himself on at half-time and turned the game. You were that close to the pitch at the Dell that I could hear him giving his instructions: "Just play it to my feet," he impressed on the players around him. Mark Hughes did just that and Gullit found himself with only the goalie to beat. He seemed to dig his boot into the turf, just enough to lob the ball over the keeper's head and into the net. Five minutes later he did it again. Chelsea went on to win 3–2.'

'It seems weird, really strange to be back,' he muses. In fact, this is his first trip back since Southampton moved to St Mary's after following up that memorable last-minute victory over Arsenal with a 1–0 win over Brighton in an end-of-season, end-of-an-era friendly. It had been against a team called Brighton United that Southampton had played their first game here in September 1898; and now the Seagulls had flown along the south coast for the very last game. Afterwards the fans flocked on to the pitch, some in search of souvenirs. 'I've still got a patch of turf in my lawn,' Dave admits.

That turf might have been a little on the damp side when it was wrenched from its roots. In his book *The Football Grounds of England and Wales* Simon Inglis describes a painting of The Dell in 1889 showing 'a tranquil pond in sunshine, surrounded by trees, with two small ducks gliding over the water . . . It cost one George Thomas £10,000 to develop the site, his first task being to reduce the pond to a series of underground streams.' Dave, the trained surveyor, was always well aware that the pitch was considerably lower than ground level. 'That's why it was called The Dell and that's why it used to get quite boggy. During the war it was bombed and the turf was completely flooded.'

If the pitch was low down, the terraces could be quite high – disproportionately so in the case of what became known as the Chocolate Boxes. These were basically terraces raised on stilts above those standing at the Milton Road end of the ground, and they came into being to meet demand in the post-war years when attendances here were rising, as they were all over the country.

But The Dell's highest ever attendance was as recent as 8 October 1969, when 31,044 squeezed in to see Saints lose 3–0 to a Manchester United side that included George Best and Bobby Charlton. 'I was there,' Dave assures me. 'There were thousands of people queuing outside on those very narrow pavements. We only got in because my mate's dad had a box with him for one of the kids to stand on. It gave him a bit of leverage. Every time he tapped someone on the back of the knees with it, they'd let him past. We just followed.'

They stood, as usual, on the terrace under the East Stand. Unbeknown to Dave, the girl who would later become his wife was somewhere behind him at the top of the terrace. 'All Penny could see was Georgie Best's ankles,' he recounts. 'She was 10 at the time and the stand came down so far over the terraces that there was only a comparatively narrow slit to peer through. That's how badly designed the ground was.' Not surprisingly, perhaps, Penny insisted on a seat when they went together to Portsmouth as a married couple on 27 February 1984. 'It meant that I had to start queuing at The Dell's ticket office at six that morning,' Dave recalls. 'It was worth it, mind you. We won 1–0 in front of 36,000 at Fratton Park. Steve Moran got the only goal in the 89th minute.'

Moran wasn't the only one who scored that day. 'Andrew, our eldest son, was born exactly nine months later,' Dave reveals. 'I remember John Motson saying on Match of the Day: "It's the game's last knockings." I thought "Oh no, it wasn't."'

The product of that union is 27 now. He has a first-class honours degree in politics – from Portsmouth, would you believe – and is guitarist in a band called the Munroe Effect. He's still a fervent Saints fan who is probably more nostalgic for The Dell than his dad. 'I miss the smell of smoke and pies overlaid with second-hand beer and Bovril,' he says. 'And I miss the intensity of the atmosphere that enabled us to punch above our weight as a club. Yes, the ground was ridiculously haphazard in the way it was put together, but you felt so close to the pitch that you could hear every tackle and swear word. I remember Kevin Davies tracking back and putting Beckham over the touchline and into the front row. The atmosphere was intimidating for those players used to performing on the big stage.'

It became less intimidating as the 1990s wore on and the legal requirement for all-seater stadia eventually reduced The Dell's capacity to not much more than 15,000. St Mary's can cater for more than twice that figure in comparative comfort – just as well now the Saints are back in the Premier League. And apart from being close to the club's origins, it's not far out of the city centre and close to the wharfs of this maritime town. Ted Bates's statue captures Mr Southampton not in shirt, shorts and boots but in jacket, shirt and tie, which is how most fans would remember him. It's a considerable improvement on the first effort, taken down by the club after supporters complained that it bore a marked resemblance to the comedian Jimmy Krankie.

There is no statue to Matt Le Tissier, as far as I can see. Plenty of time for that. For now most followers of the Saints have the image of the goals he scored and the pleasure he gave them firmly lodged in their memories. Not least that last-minute winner against Arsenal that said goodbye to The Dell in the style of a club that has regularly punched above its weight.

THE DEN

Barry Whale met his second wife Corinne 21 years ago – at Selhurst Park of all places, home of Crystal Palace. It was at one of many social functions that Barry organised in his former capacity as chairman of the Sainsbury's staff association. On their first date, he had a confession to make. 'The only thing is, Corinne,' he muttered falteringly, 'I'm a Millwall supporter.'

Her reaction was not quite what he expected. 'So am I,' she beamed with joyful incredulity.

Barry takes up the story: 'We soon discovered that we'd been standing near each other on the same terrace and had probably got on the same coaches to away matches without even knowing it. My first wife hated anything to do with football, but Corinne loves it. Millwall in particular.' It was to be a marriage made in heaven – or at least in the club's former home, The Den, which wasn't quite the same thing, as any visiting supporter would confirm. Its location, Cold Blow Lane, was aptly named. A chill of apprehension jangled the nerves of the most fearless fans as they set foot on New Cross Gate station and prepared to walk warily towards the ground. 'Cold Blow Lane on a dark, wet night might be a perfect setting for a *Jack the Ripper* horror film; dry ice wafting about the cobbled streets and under the low tunnels,' wrote Simon Inglis in

Football Grounds of England and Wales. 'There were mysterious yards full of scrap, malodorous goings-on behind high fences, tower blocks looming in the distance, even old tram lines still embedded in the roads. They knew what they were dealing with when they called it Cold Blow Lane.'

Things have changed a bit since that was written in 1985. Eight years later, Millwall upped sticks and moved along the road to The 'new' Den, a ground with considerably improved facilities and a much better outlook for visitors. They're no longer penned into a corner, their view obstructed by the base of the floodlights and a six-foot-high metal fence, painted bright yellow.

The new ground is in Bermondsey; the old one in New Cross. Each is a few hundred yards either side of a busy road that was once the Surrey

DOCKERS GET A BETTER VIEW OF THE MATCH AROUND THE EARLY 50s.

'The bog standard concrete terraces, high-wired against crowd invasion, had a touch of East Berlin to them. The muddy tunnels from the car park were pure Clockwork Orange. the loudspeakers always beat out the same belligerent message as you filed into the ground. "Let them come, let them come, let them all come down to the Den . . . We'll only have to beat them again." and the wonder of Cold Blow Lane and the old, demolished Den in the seventies and eighties was just that. There may only have been six or seven thousand there most Saturdays as the Lions oscillated between leagues, but folk memories of the sixties and 59 home games won on the trot were still strong. 'No-one likes us, no-one likes us... We don't care' wasn't your ordinary chant. It often came filled with implied menace as travelling fans huddled in their cramped little enclosure.

'The pitch – that wiring notwithstanding – was so damned close to the tough guys baying abuse. Intimidation often worked OK.

Canal. Millwall itself lies across the river in the Isle of Dogs, and the club played at various grounds around that part of the old London docks before moving to The Den in 1910. The crowd was fiercely partisan from the start, even in the era when it was considered good form to applaud enterprising football by the opposition – hence the Lions' roar and the Lions' den. Rarely in the field of footballing conflict has so much noise been generated by so few over so many generations.

Barry, now 66, first went to the old Den when he was four. He stood at the Ilderton Road end. Or rather he sat on his father's shoulders, recently vacated by his older brother. Dad was a sheet metal worker and 'a bit of a tiddler' according to his son. Certainly he would have been dwarfed by some of the beefy dockers around him, bawling their all for the Millwall cause.

'It must have been quite intimidating,' I suggest to Corinne, who was 10 when she started coming here with friends in 1959.

'It was at first, but you soon got to know everyone around you and there was a real camaraderie.' In other words, it was us against them, Millwall against the world. 'No one likes us, we don't care,' as the fans would eventually sing. The club had left the Isle of Dogs many decades previously, but there was still an insularity about The Den – or the 'Dirty Den' as it was branded by Fleet Street in the worst days of football hooliganism.

No club attracted worse headlines. Barry, a 'diamond geezer' if ever there was one, remembers looking on in horror during an FA Cup quarter-final against Ipswich in 1978. 'We were 6–1 down and the lads

'Why is the New Den, a few hundred cold blows away, so different? Because it's an anywhere ground with neat blue seats and no sense of time or place. The songs and the threats are much the same, but the atmosphere and the memories are gone. You wouldn't find Benny Fenton, a magician of a manager, howling "Boot the bloody thing over the stand" at Barry Kitchener as the lads hung on for a cup win. You couldn't replicate the hoots of laughter when Jimmy Carter, our fastest left-winger, returned from the summer break and what the programme called his body-strengthening diet a stone heavier and five yards slower. You can't – thankfully – hear the racist taunts bawled out at even our own black Lions like Phil Walker. The ghost of burly, puffing Harry Cripps is old and cherished and in no way new.

'The great, fond-remembered Den had something neither re-buildable nor transportable. It was cramped, congealing, increasingly decrepit. It probably had to go. But what went with it, demolished, lost, was the hunch of collar turned up against the chill winds from Docklands, the undeleted expletives of matches turned sour, the shared moments of raw life and crude humour. The Den was an uncanny blend of an area, the people who lived there, and a dream of glory. No-one liked us. But we still went there.'

around us behind the goal must have thought they'd got nothing to lose. They all seemed to have broken noses and cauliflower ears and they just steamed into the Ipswich supporters. A lot of people were hurt that day,' he adds with a shudder. 'It meant that the decent Millwall supporters were branded with everyone else. Whenever we travelled away, we were treated like social lepers.'

Corinne was brought up near the old ground, the daughter of a Covent Garden porter who later became a black cab driver. 'He once brought us a flask of coffee, laced with brandy, at three in the morning when we queued all night for tickets for a cup tie against West Ham,' she recalls. 'I would have been 15 or 16 at the time.'

She would go on to work, eventually, for the British Council before becoming a barrister's secretary. The Whales now live in Bexleyheath in very different surroundings from the ones she grew up in. 'There's not much of it left now,' she says as we stroll from New Cross Station first to the new Den and then on to the old. 'My old primary school's still there and that's the building where we used to have to go for a bath,' pointing to a handsome Victorian pile that now appears to be largely occupied by a windscreen replacement depot.

As for the old Den itself, that's now a large housing estate, mainly of three- or four-storey flats. Some are social housing, some privately owned. We navigate our way through with the help of Philip O'Halloran, 59, a bursar at an independent school who was the only Millwall supporter at his own Catholic school in Bexleyheath back in the 1960s.

LONDON BOROUGH OF LEWISHAM

On this site stood
The Den.
Legendary home of
Millwall Football Club
from 1910 - 1993

MILLWALL F.C.

PLAQUE ON THE SITE OF THE OLD DEN.

I blame the parents – in this case his father, who just happened to be in the diplomatic service at the Foreign Office. It seems doubtful that his expertise in diplomacy would have been much use during tense moments on the terraces of the old Den. But, having been born in nearby Deptford, he was a regular at both grounds from 1926 until he died, just after a 1–0 victory over Luton, in 2001.

Well over 10 years later, we're standing where the old centre circle used to be. It's now a tarmac track with some garages on one side and flats on the other. February is not yet over, but the air has the warmth of spring and a tree looks as though it's about to burst into blossom at any moment. Yes, trees. Some people can remember when it was all scrap yards round here. There are even what look suspiciously like palm trees outside the comparatively posh houses opposite what used to be the Cold Blow Lane turnstiles.

We stroll on to the New Cross Road, find a pub and I sit back with a pint of London Pride, listening to their reminiscences. Philip remembers the side that won promotion to the old First Division in the late 1980s and did OK for a while with Teddy Sheringham and Tony Cascarino up

front. 'We were top of the League for a whole week in October 1988,' he says. Corinne remembers Eamon Dunphy, who played for the club from 1965 to 1974 before carving out another career as a writer and broadcaster. 'Tricky midfielder and a good bloke,' Barry puts in. 'He was best man at my cousin's wedding,' he adds. Then he remembers huge family Christmas parties in Peckham, followed by a trip to the Boxing Day match at The Den with anything up to 24 male relatives.

And they all remember Harry Cripps, the combative full-back who led the charge from 1964 to 1967 as the Lions went on a run of 59 League matches unbeaten at home. Cripps himself once recalled: 'The crowd really used to intimidate the opposition. I remember marking Frannie Lee when he was playing for Bolton and, after a few minutes, he said to me: "Ain't you popular with the crowd?" I said "Yeah, but if you don't come in my half you'll be all right." He didn't really come near me for the whole game after that.'

Now Lee was no shrinking violet, as Norman Hunter would confirm. But even the most fearless of players looked forward to a trip down Cold Blow Lane with as much relish as their fans.

THE LAST EVER GAME AT THE DEN 8TH MAY 1993, VERSUS BRISTOL ROVERS.

EASTVILLE

Fresh flowers used to bloom behind each goal at Eastville at the beginning and end of every season. Those semi-circular beds, tended by the groundsman, were among several quirks that made Bristol Rovers' former ground distinctive. The predominant aroma on the terraces, however, was not floral; it was gaseous.

There was a gas holder nearby and what it emitted tended to overwhelm the more traditional smells of old football terraces – damp macs, beery breath, Bovril, fried onions and dodgy toilets. Those flowers must have been particularly hardy perennials.

'They certainly weren't red roses,' says long-time supporter Dennis Payter, who writes a column on Rovers in the local paper and several pages in the club programme. 'And I don't think you could get roses with blue and white quarters,' he adds, referring to the unusual shirts worn by Rovers and the more conventional red of their local rivals, Bristol City. It was City fans who first dubbed Eastville 'the Gas' and their supporters 'the Gasheads' – a derogatory nickname worn as a nostalgic badge of pride by Rovers loyalists ever since they departed their beloved home in 1986 and embarked on a lengthy period of exile.

Rovers would seem to be aptly named. After 10 years sharing Twerton Park with Bath City, 18 miles away, they moved back to Bristol –

though not into a ground of their own. Not immediately anyway. At first they were tenants of the local rugby club at their Memorial Ground. But in 1998, in an extraordinary reversal of fortunes, Rovers became the owners of what is now the Memorial Stadium and since then Bristol RFC have paid them rent. Plans for both clubs to move to a new stadium on land owned by the University of the West of England are, at the time of writing, dependent on Sainsbury's getting planning permission to build on a ground that was originally laid out to commemorate Bristol rugby players killed in the First World War.

Older rugby followers will have their own feelings about that. As for the round-ball game, so often its financial future seems to be tied up with what has become the nation's other great pastime: shopping. As Dennis's BMW approaches the site of his beloved Eastville, we can see below us the branch of Ikea that covers what used to be the pitch, and probably a bit more. This was, after all, one of the smallest playing surfaces in the League, measuring 110 yards by 70. The greyhound

1958-9 MATCH AGAINST SCUNTHORPE WITH THE FLOWER BEDS CLEARLY IN VIEW.

track that had encircled it since the 1930s had been expanded to accommodate speedway in 1977.

By that time the air pollution hovering over Eastville must have been approaching levels in industrial China. Apart from leaking gas, there were the exhaust fumes from high-powered motorbikes as well as endless streams of traffic on the M32 flyover, linking Bristol City centre with the M4. A ground that had started life in 1896–97, bordered by a river, watercress meadows and the 13 arches of a Great Western Railway viaduct, had been transformed – and not entirely for the better.

'It's still where my great memories are buried, though,' says Dennis as we prepare to exit on Junction 3 after passing the hard shoulder where so many cars used to mysteriously break down on match days. 'I was 10 in 1957 when I saw my first match here,' he goes on. 'I just missed our best-ever win the previous season when we beat the Busby Babes 4–0 in the FA Cup. United won the League that year and they had their best players out that day, apart from Duncan Edwards.'

Ask him about his favourite Rovers player and, like any supporter of his generation, he'll home in on Geoff Bradford. He was a one-club man

ROB ORLEDGE, 66
Former second row forward for Bath RFC and Bristol

'I was 10 when Manchester United came to Eastville in 1956. My dad was six foot three and he picked me up. Then I was passed over people's heads all the way to the front of the terrace on the south side of the ground. By that time I was playing wing-half for Somerset schoolboys and my favourite players were also wing halves – Norman Sykes of Rovers and Duncan Edwards of United and England. I remember being devastated that Edwards wasn't playing that day. But the atmosphere was just amazing, with over 35,000 in the ground, and so was the result. Beating that great side 4–0 was something I'll never forget. Pity we lost to Fulham in the next round.'

and the club's all-time leading scorer with 242 goals in 15 seasons. Known as 'Rip' (Van Winkle) because he had a habit of taking a nap before matches, Bradford also made the England team for one game only. 'But he was playing alongside players of the calibre of Tom Finney, Jackie Milburn and Nat Lofthouse,' says Dennis proudly.

Coming back to the site of the old ground is evidently a depressing experience. 'I've said to my wife if ever she wants to go to Ikea, we'll go to the one in Walsall or Cardiff. I've never set foot in this one and I don't intend to.'

Club historian Mike Jay feels much the same. 'They promised to put up a plaque to commemorate Eastville, but they never have,' he says when we finally track him down in Tesco's car park – one of several in what is now a vast expanse of retail outlets. At the far end of one of the car parks is the Eastville Club, what Mike calls 'the last reminder of the ground'. He adds: 'The players used to go there in the days when they'd have a few pints after training.' And at one time the training ground was all of a few hundred yards away, on a cindered patch of waste ground behind the old Muller Road End.

The other side of the ground was where the hardcore Rovers fans gathered. It was known as the Tote End, having acquired a betting totaliser in 1935. The River Frome flows by on what was once the south side of the ground. It flooded regularly at one time, notably in November 1950, when the Eastville pitch disappeared under several feet of water.

Any inherent dampness failed to stop the South Stand going up in flames after a fire started there mysteriously on a Sunday evening in August 1980. Eastville would never be the same again. Not only had

the administrative offices and changing rooms been destroyed; the ground was now completely open on one side and the noise from that motorway flyover seemed even more intrusive.

Crucially, the insurance money didn't go to the football club because they didn't own the ground. Hadn't done since 1940, when chairman Fred Ashmead took the unilateral decision to sell it for a mere £12,000 to the Bristol Greyhound Racing Association. No games were played here for the duration of the Second World War. Rovers would have gone bust were it not for a £3,000 cash injection in 1944 from their new owners, led by the managing director, one Constantine Augustus Lucy Stevens, and John Patrick Hare – a particularly appropriate surname for the secretary of a greyhound stadium.

Sizeable crowds in the post-war years kept the club afloat, but Rovers would never rise higher than the old Division Two. Eastville became a venue for the rising talents of players on their way up, such as Larry Lloyd and Gary Mabbutt, and ageing stars on their way down, such as Mick Channon and Alan Ball.

After the fire of 1986, the club limped on at the old place for a few more seasons before the pressures of paying rent for a much-damaged ground that they couldn't afford to repair made moving on inevitable. Bath beckoned. The final game on home turf produced a 1–1 draw against Chesterfield in May 1986. An auction followed. 'I've still got four seats from the North Stand in my garden,' Dennis confides. 'Rather symbolically, two of them have already rotted away. My wife said "Why don't you paint them green to blend in?" To which I replied: "They're blue and they always will be."'

Green seats in a garden, indeed. Whatever next? Red roses?

EMORI
OF
OVERS F
L RUGBY
USE) TERRACE ONLY
SFERS

MATCH
18

FEETHAMS

Doug Embleton, founder of the Darlington Supporters' Trust, climbs out of his car and, for a moment, we gaze up at the standard white struts protruding from the exterior of a cantilevered stand at a typical modern football stadium. 'I hate this ground,' he suddenly blurts out.

However, he loves Darlington Football Club and we've each shelled out our £10 to purchase advance tickets for tonight's match against Luton Town. Paying at the turnstiles when you arrive is not an option, apparently, although the likelihood of the game being sold out is about as remote as 'Darlo' some day qualifying for the European Champions League.

The Darlington Arena – or the Northern Echo Arena, as it was dubbed in its most recent incarnation – could hold around 25,000. Yet tonight's crowd is officially announced as 1,382. You don't have to be a mathematical genius to work out that there are over 23,000 empty seats for a match against a team riding high in the Blue Square Premier League. We all sit huddled in one stand while the other three remain virtually empty. I'm willing to bet that there's hardly an adult home fan present who doesn't wish he or she was back at the much cosier and more intimate Feethams, the club's home for 120 years until they were

uprooted in 2003, not so much to the edge of town as some distance from its southern borders.

As if to confirm my hunch, Doug muses: 'I was just remembering the way that flocks of Canada geese used to stand out against the floodlights at the South Park end of the ground as they flew home at dusk on a Saturday.' Feethams tends to evoke lyrical images. There was nothing standard or typical about it. There are, after all, few grounds bordered by a river, parkland and a cricket ground. Trees were much in evidence and nobody would have been too surprised to glimpse the occasional squirrel scuttling across the terraces.

The cricket ground is still there. Football fans used to enter through its eccentrically grand 'twin towers', almost a theme-park parody of the old gateway to Wembley Stadium, and walk around the boundary en route to the game. 'At the beginning and end of each season,

DARLINGTON FANS ARRIVING FOR THE FIRST SUNDAY FOOTBALL LEAGUE GAME AGAINST MANSFIELD TOWN.
FANS PAYING ON THE GATE TO GO THROUGH TO FEETHAMS VIA THE CRICKET PITCH, 15TH FEBRUARY 1981.

STOP PRESS: SINCE MY VISIT, THE NORTHERN ECHO DARLINGTON ARENA HAS BEEN MOTHBALLED. THE CLUB IS NOW RUN BY A COMMUNITY COMPANY CALLED DARLINGTON FC 1883 AND PLAYS ITS HOME GAMES AT BISHOP AUCKLAND'S HERITAGE PARK - EVEN FURTHER AWAY FROM FEETHAMS.

there might be a cricket match in progress,' Doug recalls. 'And after the football was over, you could sit down with a beer from the pavilion bar and unwind while watching a few overs.'

Darlington Cricket Club has hosted Durham county matches and still plays in the extremely competitive North Yorkshire and South Durham League. One end boasts what must be the league's widest sightscreen in the form of the light-painted wall right across the back of the 'Tin Shed', the terrace that used to harbour the most voluble Darlo supporters. It's the only part of the old football ground still standing. And a sorry sight it is when viewed from what used to be the pitch, now a depressing expanse of waist-high weeds and boggy wasteland, strewn with lager and cider cans as well as the occasional battered cricket ball. 'You find hypodermic needles in the bushes as well,' I've been told by Doug's fellow Feethams champion Shaun Campbell as we tour the site in the early evening before the Luton match. The uplifting sound of birdsong at dusk can't compensate for the desolation around us.

But Shaun, 50, is fiercely opposed to plans by the cricket club to sell the land to developers and cover the old ground with 146 houses. 'Feethams was left in trust to the townsfolk in the 1920s with a covenant specifying that it should be used for sporting purposes,' he insists.

But surely Darlington FC can't come back here and rebuild the ground, I point out. After all, the club is in administration and has just been relegated again.

Shaun is only too well aware of that. He and Doug were the prime movers in the Darlington Football Club Rescue Group that somehow raised £50,000 at extremely short notice to stop the club going out of business altogether early in 2012. What he wants is for the local authority to step in and preserve the site as a sporting academy for the young people of Darlington. He also wants Feethams to be recognised as a site of international importance. 'This was the home

ANDY BELL, 32
BBC Tees journalist

'I was taken to Feethams when I was nine or ten. I'd already been to big grounds such as St James's Park and Anfield, so it seemed very tight. It was also surprisingly loud. There were only four or five thousand people there but the noise they made scared me.'

RICHARD TATE, 41
Joiner

'My first game at Feethams was back in 1986 and we beat Swansea 6–0. Now they're in the Premier League and we're in the Blue Square North. George Reynolds did well for us at first, but he should have waited until we'd gone up a few divisions before building this stadium.'

of the world's first ever black professional footballer,' he points out. 'Arthur Wharton started his career here in the mid-1880s.' Almost another 100 years would pass before the first black player, Viv Anderson, was picked for England.

Wharton played in goal for Darlington, but he was just as likely to pop up in the opposition penalty area at regular intervals in the full knowledge that he could race back again quicker than anyone else on the field. After all, he was the fastest man on earth at the time, being the world record holder over 100 yards. 'There were times when he'd score more than once in a game,' I'm assured by Shaun, who has a shrine to Wharton at the imposing emporium above a former billiard hall where he sells African sculptures and artefacts. He's also the man behind a campaign to raise money for a statue to his hero at the heart of this pleasant town that owes much of its development in the Victorian era to local Quaker families. That's why the football club is also known as the Quakers.

Heaven knows what those pillars of probity would have made of the goings-on here when convicted safe-cracker George Reynolds bought the club at the end of the 20th century. It was Reynolds who initially bailed out Darlo financially. 'In his first season here he funded a very good team,' says Doug. 'We very narrowly missed out on promotion. He'd also reduced entrance prices at Feethams and the crowds were up.'

Good old George, then. He became quite a popular figure among Quakers fans. Not for long, however. After promising Premier League football within five years, he made the mistake of building a sizeable stadium without putting together a team remotely capable of filling it. Needless to say, he named the new ground after himself. Yes, this white-strutted white elephant was initially known as the Reynolds Stadium. Again, not for long. The year after it opened for business, its founder was stopped by police who discovered £500,000 in bank notes in the boot of his car. Initially arrested for money-laundering, he later pleaded guilty to tax evasion.

THE WASTELAND IN FRONT OF WHAT USED TO BE THE TIN SHED WHERE THE MORE VOLUBLE DARLINGTON SUPPORTERS STOOD.

Meanwhile, Darlington FC was left to pick up the pieces. The club didn't move out of the basement division until 2010 – and then it was in the wrong direction. They dropped out of the Football League altogether. 'Because George had been a Sunderland fan initially, I think he thought Darlington people would turn out in large numbers to watch football,' Doug suggests. 'We tried to tell him that, historically, our gates at Feethams were around the three and a half thousand level.'

There have been much bigger crowds than that, however. Notably in 1960 when a 3–2 win over West Ham in the League Cup was followed by a 2–1 defeat by Bolton, Nat Lofthouse and all, in front of over 21,000 spectators. 'It not only broke the attendance record but also the *Guinness Book of Records* mark for the most people in one place participating in synchronised breathing,' Doug deadpans. At my instigation, he's reminiscing in a pub near Shaun's shop shortly before the Luton game.

Doug would have been 13 in 1960, which turned out to be quite a year for Darlington. An FA Cup tie against Hull was petering out in the 89th minute with the home side 1–0 down when Darlo's Bobby Baxter put what Doug calls 'a speculative lob' just over the crossbar. One of his mates from the local grammar school leaned over the fence of the brand new Tin Shed terrace and pushed the ball back to the Hull keeper under the back of the net. On seeing the goalie retrieving the ball, the referee promptly blew for a goal and set in train no fewer than four replays. Hull finally settled the tie with a 3–0 victory at Ayresome Park, Middlesbrough. This was also the year when the first floodlights went up at Feethams and the West Stand burnt down as a result of a fault in the cabling.

They could have done with those floodlights two seasons previously when a Cup tie against Chelsea finished in near-darkness. Then again, perhaps not. As it turned out, Darlington scored three times in the murky gloom of extra time to clinch a 4–1 victory that passed into

SHAUN CAMPBELL AT HIS SHRINE TO ARTHUR WHARTON, THE FIRST BLACK FOOTBALLER IN THE ENGLISH GAME, WHO PLAYED IN GOAL FOR DARLINGTON.

local folklore. The match was played on a Wednesday afternoon and the packed terraces suggest that there were a lot of grandmothers' funerals in town that day. Young Doug wagged off school with a faked sore throat. He finished the match with a real one, having bellowed himself hoarse along with every other fan of the home side. Pathe News was there to record the event and crowds queued round the block to watch the highlights at the Regal.

Soon it will be time to drag ourselves off to the Luton match, but for those of us not driving there's time for one more pint and the opportunity to listen to a few more Darlo memories. Of old-fashioned centre-forwards such as Bill Tulip, who banged in 36 goals in 44 matches in the late fifties. Of modern strikers such as Marco Gabbiadini, who scored over 50 goals in two seasons at the end of the nineties. Of the days when players often worked on Saturday mornings before a match – shoeing horses down the pit in the case of centre-half and colliery blacksmith Ron Greener and filling teeth in the case of wing-half and local dentist Lance Robson.

By now I'm beginning to wish we could stay in the pub and carry on talking. But we have paid a tenner a head for these tickets. Darlington v Luton calls. And, as it turns out, it's not such a bad match as 1–1 draws go. The Quakers are awarded a penalty in the last minute of injury time. Cue another good save by the Luton keeper to groans all round. Just to rub it in we have to wait 20 minutes to get out of the car park before embarking on the lengthy drive back into town. There may be only 1,382 people here but every one of them has had to come by car.

Had the game been played at Feethams, our appointment with Darlington's finest curry house would have come about considerably earlier – as long as it would have taken for a short stroll into town after circumnavigating a cricket pitch and passing through the twin towers.

FELLOWS PARK

On the way from Bescot Stadium station to Walsall FC's current ground is a path inlaid here and there with slabs inscribed with elaborate lettering, perhaps by some community artist with a deadpan sense of humour. One of them reads: 'Deep peace of the quiet earth and the shining stars to you.'

There are other messages in a similar vein, all of which seem somewhat at odds with the surroundings. Above our heads thunder six lanes of heavy traffic on the M6 flyover.

A mere four lanes separate the ground from a car park commandeered for match-day parking. It's Saturday morning and there's a lunchtime kick-off today against Rochdale in a ground that looks a bit dated, despite being only 22 years old. A riot of conflicting signage afflicts the eyes as various sponsors jostle for attention. Incidentally, this is now the Banks's rather than the Bescot Stadium. Well, at least the main sponsor is a Black Country brewery rather than a Middle Eastern airline or a Chinese chain of casinos.

In an hour or two's time, season-ticket holder Steve Best will take his seat in the upper reaches of the Tile Choice Stand. But first he has agreed to convey me a short distance down the dual carriageway to the site of his beloved Fellows Park, Walsall's home from 1896 until 1990.

For the first 34 of those years it was known simply as Hillary Street. Only in 1930 did it acquire the name of its then chairman, one HL Fellows.

His legacy now lies buried somewhere under a Morrison's supermarket. Steve's black Audi comes to rest in a car park the size of the Isle of Wight as he points out the only nod to the past on the outside of the building – a clock over the entrance, designed to look like a football. Inside, however, one wall is graced by some evocative historical photos of Fellows Park.

On a bench in front of one such sepia gem sit a man and a woman, both of whom are nothing short of obese. He is studying the *Daily Star*; she is flicking through some magazine full of svelte celebrities. When I ask if I could have a quick look at the photo behind them, they obligingly shift their considerable weight onto one enormous buttock apiece. Without saying a word, they carry on reading while I take

ALLY BROWN OF WALSALL IS TACKLED BY MARK LAWRENSON OF LIVERPOOL DURING THE WALSALL VERSUS LIVERPOOL MILK CUP SEMI-FINAL 2ND
LEG MATCH PLAYED AT FELLOWS PARK, WALSALL ON THE 14TH FEBRUARY 1984. LIVERPOOL WON THE MATCH 2-0 AND 4-2 ON AGGREGATE.

'ARSENAL, THE RICH, THE CONFIDENT, THE LEAGUE LEADERS, THE £30,000 ARISTOCRATS, AGAINST A LITTLE MIDLAND THIRD DIVISION TEAM THAT COST £69 IN ALL. ARSENAL TRAIN ON OZONE, BRINE-BATHS, CHAMPAGNE, GOLF AND ELECTRICAL MASSAGE IN AN ATMOSPHERE OF PRIMA DONNA SELFISHNESS. THEY OWN £87 WORTH OF FOOTBALL BOOTS. WALSALL MEN EAT FISH AND CHIPS AND DRINK BEER, AND THE ENTIRE RUNNING EXPENSES OF THE CLUB THIS SEASON HAVE BEEN £75.'

A newspaper preview of Walsall's 1933 cup tie against Arsenal

advantage of the space created to study a revealing shot of Walsall players tucking into oysters before their fabled 2–0 victory over Arsenal in the third round of the FA Cup, 1933. Managed by Herbert Chapman, Arsenal were the Barcelona of their day: simply the best club side on the world. Which makes you wonder about the power of oysters to boost the ability to score.

Unfortunately, only 11,189 were there to see one of the greatest cup upsets of all time, despite Mr Fellows and his fellow directors having splashed out to put up a roof over the 'popular side' terracing to complement the recently finished Main Stand opposite. They'd also put the prices up, which may help to explain why the ground was only half full. Another 28 years would pass before Fellows Park enjoyed a record attendance of 25,453, by which time the back wall of Orgills Laundry had been replaced by a small terrace for away fans. The Saddlers beat Newcastle 1–0 that day in Division Two.

Steve, 42 and a graphic designer, started coming here in the late 1970s, after a brief flirtation with Villa Park, a few stops down the line. 'My granddad was a Villa fan,' he explains. 'But, as his health deteriorated, he didn't like being in big crowds and brought me here instead. Somehow I felt more comfortable at Walsall. I used to stand behind the low wall, just to the side of the goal at the front of the Hillary Street end. I reckon it must have been round about here.' He pauses for a moment in a gap between checkouts nine and ten before continuing: 'My second cousin used to stand next to me and I remember him being hit in the face by a fierce shot that was just wide. He had to be lifted over the wall by a St John's Ambulance man before being taken down the tunnel for treatment. I went with him and for me it was quite a thrill to go down the place where the players ran out.'

His hero at the time was Alan Buckley, who had rejoined the club from First Division Birmingham City as player-manager for a record £175,000 in 1979. Before his brief sojourn into the top flight, he had rewritten the Walsall record books by scoring over 20 goals in each of his previous five seasons with the club. His final total was 205 goals in 484 games. In 1986, however, he was sacked as manager by incoming chairman Terry Ramsden, a City whizz-kid who arrived at Fellows Park by helicopter promising promotion and a free Christmas turkey to every pensioner in the ground. Alas, Ramsden did not survive the crash of the Japanese securities market the following year and, for a while, it looked as though Walsall FC might not survive either.

The ground had become increasingly dilapidated. Four years previously a wall had collapsed at the Laundry End – or rather the Railway End as it had become known by then. Liverpool fans were gathered there to watch their side win a Milk Cup semi-final replay 2–0. 'As soon as Ian Rush put them ahead, down came the wall,' Steve recalls. 'Twenty-four people were injured and I remember Graeme Souness helping out by carrying a child to safety.'

PHIL MACKMAN, 67
Sales manager

'As a child just after the war, I lived with my grandparents close to Fellows Park. A lot of people came on bikes in those days and my granddad would let them park in the front garden for three (old) pence a time. It kept him in beer money for the rest of the week.'

PAUL DAVIS, 50
Roofer

'I was watching *Coronation Street* one night when Reg Holdsworth, manager of Fresco's, announced that he was going down to Walsall in the West Midlands for a supermarket opening. Next thing we knew, Fellows Park had been sold. After that I always assumed that Fresco was just a stage name for Morrison's.'

Luckily, nobody was killed. There would be enough deaths at football grounds elsewhere as that grim decade wore on. By the end of the 1980s, Walsall were being run by a consortium of businessmen, including Leeds United board member Peter Gilman. It was his construction company that was eventually granted the contract to build the new ground on the site of an old Severn Trent sewage works. Fans were somewhat underwhelmed when the final design turned out to be a straight copy of Scunthorpe's recently completed Glanford Park. But at least Walsall had avoided having to share St Andrews with Birmingham, the proposal put forward by Ramsden's predecessor Ken Wheldon.

When I ask Steve if he misses Fellows Park, he nods reflectively. 'It's in the soul,' he muses. 'You had no great expectations coming here, except to have a laugh with those around you and the occasional pleasant surprise, like beating Sheffield Wednesday one Boxing Day and – even better – thumping Birmingham 5–0.' He pauses again before adding: 'Mind you, the place was a bit of a dump. The gents' toilet was primitive and right next door to the place where they sold tea and Bovril. If I close my eyes, I can still smell it now.'

Not a pleasant thought to conjure with, especially as we're now in the Morrison's café and a disproportionate number of customers are tucking into full English breakfasts as lunchtime approaches. It's also not too long to kick-off. Soon Steve is heading for the Tile Choice Stand while I find myself trudging back along the path of deep peace and quiet under the M6 flyover.

WALSALL STRIKER ALISTAIR BROWN SHOOTS WATCHED BY LIVERPOOL DEFENDER MARK LAWRENSON DURING THEIR LEAGUE CUP SEMI-FINAL 2ND LEG, SPONSORED BY THE MILK MARKETING BOARD, AT FELLOWS PARK, WALSALL, 14TH FEBRUARY 1984. LIVERPOOL WON 4–2 ON AGGREGATE TO REACH THE FINAL.

FILBERT STREET

We pull up on Filbert Street and straight ahead of us is the sign for Lineker Road. A fitting tribute, you might think, to the *Match of the Day* presenter whose goals lit up his hometown ground before he moved on to more celebrated arenas.

Well, yes, that's what it was meant to be when Leicester City fans voted to name a new byway in a new development on the site of their old stadium after 'young Gary', as he was known when he started his career here. Trouble is that times have changed since that poll was taken in 2005. The property boom has collapsed and, although there are student flats on what used to be known as the 'double-decker' stand at the far end of the ground, there's little sign of any other building activity.

'Crappiest little street you could imagine,' mutters City's official historian John Hutchinson. After we've climbed out of his car and taken a stroll along it, I can see what he means. To the right is one of those 'temporary' car parks that looks as though it might be a fixture for some time to come. And to the left is a row of boards covered with peeling paint. 'The old centre circle was just over there,' John points out as we peer round the far end of the furthest board across a wasteland strewn with burger cartons and pizza boxes.

Beyond is another late-Victorian terraced street that not only backed onto the popular side but helped to provide access to it. 'See that house with different tiles from all the rest.' John gestures across the wasteland: 'In the 60s, the club had the ground floor replaced by turnstiles.' Presumably they asked the owners' permission? 'Leicester City were the owners. There were quite a few club houses in that terrace.'

Not enough, however, to get planning permission to demolish the street and expand that cramped terrace into a more expansive seated area. The other side of the ground had already been developed. But then the old main stand had nothing but a car park behind it. The imposing Carling Stand that replaced it towered over the rest of the ground to give Filbert Street a distinctly unbalanced appearance. 'Martin O'Neill used to call the popular side a bus shelter,' John confides. 'He always said that whenever he brought a new player to the club, he'd walk them out of the tunnel backwards so that they'd focus on the Carling.'

LEICESTER CITY VERSUS SPURS. A PARACHUTIST FLIES IN OVER THE STANDS ON FEBRUARY 18, 1921.

LEICESTER CITY VERSUS SPURS. FILBERT STREET'S HIGHEST EVER ATTENDANCE. 18TH FEBRUARY 1921.

WHEN FILBERT STREET OPENED, IN 1891, IT WAS THE HOME OF LEICESTER FOSSE FC. THEIR LAST GAME WAS A 5–1 WIN OVER LEEDS CITY ON 17 APRIL 1915. SOON AFTERWARDS, THE DECISION WAS TAKEN TO SUSPEND LEAGUE AND CUP FOOTBALL FOR THE REST OF THE FIRST WORLD WAR. BY THE TIME COMPETITIVE GAMES GOT UNDER WAY AGAIN IN 1919, LEICESTER HAD GROWN FROM A TOWN INTO A CITY AND THE NAME OF THE CLUB WAS CHANGED ACCORDINGLY.

It was completed in 1993 and demolished barely 10 years later. By that time, the club had long ago concluded that planning problems prevented expansion and the only way to get an all-seater stadium with a decent capacity was to move. The last game at Filbert Street was a 2–1 victory over Tottenham at the end of the 2001–02 season. Lineker, of course, had played for Spurs more recently than he had played for Leicester, but he was sitting in the stands applauding when the winning goal was volleyed in by Matt Piper. 'Matt used to be a pupil of mine,' says John, a former head teacher. 'He was a good lad.' Never better, one suspects, than when that winner hit the roof of the net.

The new ground was built on a former power station and is clearly visible beyond a line of electricity pylons that straddle the no-man's-land between the two sites. Close up I can see that the Foxes' new den stands on another recently named road: Filbert Way. Among the giant advertisements bedecking its exterior is one for Walkers Crisps. Until 2011, of course, it was known as the Walkers Stadium. Local company, local club – an ideal combination, you might imagine. But this is football in the 21st century and the bottom line is who can put in the most cash. So within a decade, the home of Leicester City has gone from Filbert Street to the Walkers Stadium to the King Power Stadium, named after a duty-free franchise company based in Bangkok.

It's fair to say that life has not been a bed of roses for the club, on or off the field, since they moved. After a few months in their new home, they went into administration with debts of around £50 million. Only a bail-out by a consortium led by Lineker saved them from going out of business.

No wonder so many fans look back wistfully on the good old days of the 1990s. Steve Walsh and Robbie Savage were putting in the challenges, Muzzy Izzet was creating plenty of chances and Emile Heskey was putting some of them away and selflessly laying off others. The Foxes reached Wembley seven times in nine years, first under Brian Little and then under Martin O'Neill. Four of the seven were play-offs and three were League Cup finals, two of which were won under O'Neill, in 1997 and 2000.

But when I ask John whether he misses Filbert Street, he sighs before reflecting: 'There were some great occasions at the old place. Still, if you asked me whether I'd prefer to be sitting in our current stadium or standing on a cold terrace, I think I'd opt for the King Power.' He's 62 and those terraces must have seemed a lot warmer 50 years ago when he started going to matches with the same friends that he still meets up with today. 'We were spoilt in the 60s,' he beams. 'We reached three FA Cup finals within a decade. OK, we lost the lot, but we also made it to two League Cup finals and won one of them. And we were always in the top half of the old First Division. Gordon Banks was in goal, Richie Norman in defence, Mike Stringfellow on the wing and Davie Gibson, my all-time favourite, making things happen in the middle of the park.'

LEICESTER CITY'S HIGHEST SCORER WAS ARTHUR CHANDLER, WHO BANGED IN 259 GOALS IN 303 GAMES FOR THE FOXES BETWEEN 1923 AND 1935. ONE SEASON HE SCORED 44 IN 42 GAMES. THESE DAYS HE WOULD BE WORTH CONSIDERABLY MORE THAN FERNANDO TORRES AND BE ABLE TO AFFORD A MANSION IN THE VALE OF BELVOIR. BUT DURING HIS EARLY YEARS AT THE CLUB, CHANDLER LIVED JUST ACROSS THE ROAD FROM THE GROUND IN A TWO-UP, TWO-DOWN TERRACE ON FILBERT STREET ITSELF.

Another top Leicester side would emerge in the mid-1970s. 'They played great football but never won anything,' John recalls. Mind you, Frank Worthington was worth the entrance fee and Keith Weller was great value, too. He memorably scored a hat-trick against Liverpool at Filbert Street in 1972 to give Leicester a 3–2 victory after they'd been 2–0 down. But, as he admitted in Neville Foulger's book *Farewell to Filbert Street*, the game that he'll always be remembered for was the third-round cup tie against Norwich in January 1979, when he wore tights for the first time. White tights.

Admittedly it was a freezing day and quite a few games elsewhere had been called off. All the same, it was quite a shock when he opened the box that he'd ordered from a sports shop. 'The tights were white, not black as I had expected,' he told Foulger. 'But I'd put my neck on the line by telling everyone that I was going to wear tights and I couldn't back down. I remember Jock Wallace [the manager recently arrived from Glasgow Rangers] walking in as I was putting them on, looking at me and saying: "You're not going to wear those tights, you fairy." It could have been a real nightmare, but fortunately I had a decent game and scored a goal.' Those tights had pride of place at Weller's coffee shop in Seattle until his sad death from cancer, aged 58, in 2004. He had played and coached in America during the 1980s and 90s.

Lineker had made his debut against Oldham Athletic in 1979, on another freezing January day – New Year's Day, to be precise.

Nobody watching would have predicted that 'young Gary' would go on to play for England, let alone become his country's second highest all-time scorer after Bobby Charlton. Certainly not John Williams, the sociologist at Leicester University who specialises in football-related issues. 'Lineker could hardly stand up that day, let alone demonstrate any technique,' he recalls. 'It took him a while to establish himself, but once he found his feet, he soon proved that he could finish.'

Williams is a Liverpool season-ticket holder but spent a lot of time at Filbert Street in the 1970s and 80s, working with the club on issues of racism and hooliganism. He was able to observe at close quarters the activities of Leicester's so-called 'Baby Squad', who were not as cherubic as their nickname suggests. 'They were in the terrible position of unrequited antagonism,' the academic wryly suggests. 'Leicester has a triangular relationship with Nottingham and Derby. But the Baby Squad were frustrated to discover that their opposite numbers at Forest and County seemed to hate each other more than them. Still, Filbert Street became quite an important venue at the height of the hooligan era. It's easily reachable from London, so the Chelsea, West Ham and Tottenham squads seemed to relish making the trip.'

Away fans were housed at one end of the popular side – the end closest to the terraced section below the seats on the 'double-decker', otherwise known as the Kop End. So where did the Baby Squad gather? You've guessed it: as close as possible to the visitors. 'Antagonism

FILBERT STREET'S BIGGEST CROWD WAS 47,298 FOR AN FA CUP FIFTH-ROUND TIE AGAINST SPURS ON 18 FEBRUARY 1928. MANY MORE CLAMBERED ONTO WALLS AND ROOFS TO SEE CITY GO DOWN 3–0. A FEW DAREDEVILS SHINNED UP A TELEGRAPH POLE AND SLID DOWN A DIAGONAL TELEPHONE LINE INTO A PACKED TERRACE AT THE FILBERT STREET END. ANOTHER 8,000 WERE LOCKED OUTSIDE. THE BIGGEST CROWD AT THE WALKERS-TURNED-KING-POWER STADIUM WAS 32,500 TO SEE... LEICESTER TIGERS PLAY BATH IN A HEINEKEN CUP MATCH IN 2006. LEICESTER JUST HAPPENS TO HAVE THE BEST-SUPPORTED RUGBY UNION TEAM IN THE UK. THE HIGHEST ATTENDANCE FOR FOOTBALL WAS 32,188 FOR A PRE-SEASON FRIENDLY IN JULY 2011. THE OPPONENTS? REAL MADRID. THE SCORE: 2–1 TO THE SPANIARDS.

tended to increase as you moved from left to right across the Kop,' Williams remembers. 'It was a troubled space and a very white space.'

Racist chanting was rife at most grounds in those days. So perhaps it's not surprising that, with a few exceptions, Leicester's substantial Asian population stayed away and remained under-represented until the ground closed. 'The King Power has opened things up a bit,' Williams points out. 'You see more Asian faces in the crowd now, but they're still in single figures as a percentage of the fans. This in a city that could soon have an ethnic majority.'

Female supporters, on the other hand, are well represented at the new stadium. Research by Williams and one of his former PhD students, Stacey Pope – now Dr Pope of the University of Bedford – suggests that at least a quarter of Leicester's regular home fans are women or girls.

There were also more female fans at Filbert Street than popular perceptions suggest. The sociologists have carried out interviews with women old enough to remember being on the terraces back in the 1950s and early 60s, when, as one retired community social worker put it: 'People were more careful about the way they treated each other . . . the atmosphere was sort of friendly . . . well, I didn't see any sign of people being rude or aggressive.'

A retired secretary remembered home and away fans mingling together. 'That was part of it, conversing with them. You'd say "He's a good player" or "What's so-and-so like? I've not seen him play yet" to an away supporter.'

Most supporters of that generation had lived through at least one world war and had the perspective to put football into context, as an enjoyable diversion from the hardships of everyday life. Dr Pope recently published another piece of research on 'women as new consumer fans'. The title was 'Like Pulling Down Durham Cathedral and Building a Brothel' – a direct quote from a female Foxes fan on the demolition of Filbert Street.

Now there's a thought. Never mind that comparing a block of student flats with a brothel seems a little hard on the students. Likening Filbert Street to Durham Cathedral is a bit like comparing Lineker Road, Leicester, with the Royal Crescent in Bath.

A YOUNG FAN SHOWS THEIR FEELINGS ABOUT LEAVING FILBERT STREET.

GAY MEADOW

Let's get the name out of the way first. Gay Meadow opened for business in 1910, long before the word 'gay' had acquired its current connotations. It was simply associated with frolicsome activity of any kind and the football field was laid out on the site of fairs, fêtes and festivals. Or so it is assumed.

But Shrewsbury Town's official historian, Mike Jones, has a more intriguing theory. The nearby English Bridge, rebuilt and widened in the 1920s, was first constructed in the 1770s to replace an ancient Norman toll bridge. At that time, one end was the gathering point for local prostitutes. Female ones. 'The meadow was a handy place to bring their clients and the word "gay" was applied to prostitutes in those days,' Mike suggests. A rum thought to conjure with for Town fans, who for years had to put up with tiresomely predictable homophobic abuse from visiting supporters.

Since 2007, however, their home has been Greenhous Meadow, named after nothing more spicy than the sponsor and sited amid flat fields, ring roads and roundabouts on the bland and featureless edge of town. Old-timers like Mike, still reporting for Sky TV's *Soccer Saturday* in his mid-sixties, left their hearts at that damp and rickety old ground sandwiched between the Severn and the railway line in an unusually scenic setting for football. 'We all miss it,' he admits. 'But it had fallen

into disrepair and it was always prey to flooding. The club first thought about moving in 1968, so it took them nearly 40 years.'

Well, life has a leisurely pace here in Shropshire. You could say that it meanders along like that wide, slate-grey river from which the ball had to be retrieved at regular intervals when 'Salop' were at home. 'Only lazy journalists ever call us the Shrews,' Mike insists. Back in the 1950s, when Shrewsbury were enjoying their new status as fully fledged members of the Football League, the cry would go up: 'Breathe on 'em Salop', which must rank as one of the more unusual terrace chants.

But then Gay Meadow was a most unusual ground. There can't be too many main stands offering views of a church spire ahead, a castle turret to the right and terraces of handsome Georgian properties somewhere in between. And then there was Fred Davies. No, not the manager who led them to the dizzy heights of the old League Division Two in 1993–94 and kept them there for three seasons. We're talking about his

SHREWSBURY TOWN VERSUS ARSENAL FA CUP MATCH AT GAY MEADOW,
27TH JANUARY 1968. A POLICEMAN REMOVES A SUPPORTER FROM THE CROWD.

THE MOST VOCAL SHREWSBURY SUPPORTERS USED TO GATHER AROUND THE HALFWAY LINE ON THE RIVERSIDE TERRACE. THIS WAS ALSO A MEETING POINT FOR THE SELF-APPOINTED ENGLISH BORDER FRONT, WHOSE NAME OWES MUCH TO THE CLOSE PROXIMITY OF WALES.

GAY MEADOW WITNESSED QUITE A FEW GIANT-KILLING EXPLOITS OVER THE YEARS. ONE OF THE MOST MEMORABLE HAPPENED IN 1962, THE FIRST SEASON OF THE LEAGUE CUP. SHREWSBURY KNOCKED THEN-MIGHTY EVERTON OUT IN THE QUARTER-FINALS. FINAL SCORE: 2–1 WITH BOTH GOALS FROM CENTRE-HALF PETER DOLBY, AN ENGINEERING APPRENTICE WHOSE BIKE WAS OVERTAKEN BY THE EVERTON COACH ON THE WAY TO THE GROUND.

namesake, the ball-retriever in that small, round boat known as a coracle.

Mike's features break into a broad grin at the memory. 'You had to remember that there was a weir 300 yards away and Fred had to get up a head of steam to catch up with the ball before it went over. Off he went one foggy night, increasingly desperate, until he spotted a white shape, pulled up alongside and reached out to scoop it up. To his alarm, the shape took off. He'd just disturbed a sleeping swan. Perhaps he was lucky that he wasn't attacked.'

On most occasions, Fred would return to the stadium and stroll down the touchline with the damp ball under his arm. The crowd would burst into applause and he would reclaim his seat next to the manager. 'He must have saved the club a fortune over the years,' Mike points out. 'So when decimalisation came in, they doubled his wages – from five bob to 50p a ball.'

Fred was once called upon to extend his duties during the managerial reign of former Manchester United goalkeeper and Munich hero Harry Gregg. Mike takes up the story: 'It must have been around 1969 and we were 1–0 down with 10 minutes to go. Against Chesterfield, I think it was. One of the linesmen pulled a muscle and the call went out for someone to run the line alongside the Riverside Stand. Harry nudged Fred, told him to grab that flag and raise it if the opposition scored again. Sure enough they did score, quite legitimately as it turned out. The crowd groaned, but there was Fred frantically waving the flag for offside. The ref had to go over, put his arm round him and gently overrule him.'

Fred hung up his waders in 1986 and died eight years later. His nephew took over the roll of ball retriever in chief, albeit in a proper rowing boat, until the club moved on and his services were no longer required. Today mechanical diggers are hovering over the remains of Gay Meadow. Soon it will be just another housing development. Mike looks

CHRIS SMITH, 59
Chairman of the Super Blues fundraising club

'The match I best remember was the one against Exeter in May 1979, when we beat them 4–1 and were promoted from the old Third Division under Graham Turner. I was one of 14,000 packed in and the atmosphere was electric. Thousands of us ran on the pitch to celebrate at the final whistle. I was 26 at the time.'

on with resignation before pointing out the Station End, which was so packed for a derby against Walsall in April 1961 that some spectators were accommodated on the roof. There were 18,917 wedged in that day. The capacity was some 10,000 fewer when Shrewsbury finally upped sticks and moved to the edge of town.

Ask any Salop supporter of a certain age about their favourite footballer and they're like to come up with the name of Arthur Rowley. He announced his arrival as player-manager in the 1958–59 season with 38 goals in 43 games to lead the club out of the wilderness of the Fourth Division. Not bad for a man already well into his thirties. For the next four seasons his tally was 32, 28, 23 and 24 respectively. Rowley finally called it a day in 1965, just short of his fortieth birthday, by which time he'd scored 152 goals for Shrewsbury – 99 fewer than he scored in his prime for Leicester City.

'Shot on him like a mule,' Mike recalls. 'I remember being behind the goal when he let rip with a vicious volley from close range and Watford's 17-year-old goalie pulled off one of the best saves I've ever seen. I said to the bloke next to me: "That lad will go far."' He did, too. As far as White Hart Lane and Highbury in a distinguished career that spanned Spurs and Arsenal, not to mention any number of international venues in 119 appearances for Northern Ireland. Still, it seems unlikely that Pat Jennings played at many grounds more quaintly scenic than Gay Meadow.

Not that he would have had much time to admire the view when Arthur Rowley was bearing down on goal.

COCA-COLA FOOTBALL LEAGUE TWO – PLAY-OFF SEMI-FINAL SHREWSBURY TOWN VERSUS MILTON KEYNES DONS.
SHREWSBURY TOWN FANS INVADE THE PITCH AFTER THE LAST EVER GAME AT GAY MEADOW. 15TH AUGUST 2001.

THE GOLDSTONE GROUND

Ian Chadband has witnessed many a dramatic moment in stadia throughout the world while reporting for the London *Evening Standard*, the *Sunday Times* and, more recently, for the *Daily Telegraph* in his current capacity as chief sports correspondent. But never has he seen anything quite like the scenes that followed the final whistle of the last game at the Goldstone Ground on 26 April 1997.

A Stuart Storer goal against Doncaster Rovers had been enough to offer Brighton and Hove Albion a lifeline that they successfully clung to the following week at Hereford to secure Football League status by the skin of their teeth — teeth worn down, in their supporters' case, by the constant gnawing of fingernails.

At the end of the Doncaster game, a significant portion of the capacity crowd strode on to the pitch with a purposeful air. They'd come 'tooled up'. Not to attack anyone who had made the lengthy journey from South Yorkshire. No, they simply wanted to dismantle a ground that they believed had been stolen from them by members of their own board of directors and take home a fragment or two as a souvenir. Without providing an adequate replacement, those directors had sold off the Goldstone to developers whose mechanical diggers would soon swoop like vultures over the bulldozed remains of whatever was left. And that wasn't much, according to Chadband. 'As I was filing my report

for the *Sunday Times*, I became aware that the place was being ripped apart around us. Signs were disappearing. Even toilets went. It wasn't wildly unruly, just efficient — like being on a building demolition site. And they didn't invade the press box. They just let us get on and do our jobs.'

The media, after all, had helped to expose the goings-on that had led to the destruction of the Goldstone. Gone now was the ground that had been home to Mark Lawrenson, en route to Liverpool, Jimmy Case, en route from Liverpool, Bobby Smith six months after playing for Spurs and England, and Brian Clough in a brief and undistinguished managerial interlude between Derby and Leeds. Gone, all gone.

Albion historian Tim Carder was there on that final day, as usual. 'I took a small piece of turf away,' he confides from the other side of the busy Old Shoreham Road as we watch the sun going down between DFS and

BOBBY SMITH, CENTRE-FORWARD IN THE SPURS DOUBLE-WINNING SIDE OF
1961, SIGNED FOR BRIGHTON IN MAY 1964. THEY WERE IN THE FOURTH
DIVISION AT THE TIME. THE FEE WAS £5,000 AND THE DEAL WAS FACILITATED BY
A BOOKMAKER CALLED GEORGE GUNN, LEADING TO SPECULATION THAT ALBION
HAD PAID OFF SMITH'S GAMBLING DEBTS — AN ALLEGATION THAT HE STAUNCHLY
DENIED. THE FOLLOWING SEASON, HOWEVER, HE FELL OUT WITH THE CLUB OVER
A SUNDAY NEWSPAPER ARTICLE ADMITTING THAT HE WAS A COMPULSIVE GAMBLER.
THE FORMER SPURS HERO MOVED DOWN TO HASTINGS UNITED WHILE BRIGHTON
MOVED UP TO DIVISION THREE, LARGELY THANKS TO SMITH'S CONTRIBUTION OF
19 LEAGUE GOALS IN 31 APPEARANCES.

Toys R Us. Somewhere just below that point is the rough location of the former centre circle. The retail park that replaced the old ground could be on the edge of any town or city from Newark, Notts, to Newark, New Jersey, which makes it difficult to believe that the hedge bordering it was once the back of Brighton's North Stand. 'It housed the noisiest home fans,' Tim explains before pointing beyond the drive-thru' Burger King to the location of the expansive East Terrace that ran all the way along one touchline. 'That's where I used to go. I first went there in 1965 when I was seven and climbed right to the topmost step. I couldn't get over the green of the pitch, the blue and white of the Brighton players and the red and white of Charlton. It was the most exciting event I'd witnessed in my life so far. Pity we lost 3–0.'

Like a lot of football fans of a certain generation, Tim had only watched professional football until then on a grainy black and white television. He's 55 now and for 14 years of his life he steadfastly refused to clap eyes on the assemblage of retail warehouses across the road that had crushed the soul out of his field of dreams. 'If I had to come to this part of town, I'd always find another route,' he admits. 'If someone else was driving, I'd close my eyes until we'd passed it. Only when the new stadium was finally opened at the beginning of July 2011 and we came here to unveil this heritage board could I bear to look at it for the first time.'

The board, put together by Tim to summarise the history of his former second home, is next to where we're standing on the immaculately manicured lawns of Hove Park. Behind is the Goldstone itself – a 20-ton chunk of sandstone and flint that was unearthed in September 1900, nearly 18 months before Albion played their first friendly on the ground, beating Southampton Wanderers 7–1. The rock apparently became a big attraction for Druids. It seems an odd thing to find in this

neck of the woods. But then so was a football stadium. There are none of the streets of red-brick terraces that usually cluster around those sporting relics of Victorian and Edwardian Britain. Instead there are substantial four- and five-bedroomed villas nearby, some with stained glass windows and colourfully tiled front paths. 'This isn't just Brighton,' they seem to suggest. 'This is Brighton and Hove, actually.'

Nobody, however, should underestimate the power of football to unleash passions on the south-east coast every bit as strong as those in the game's more traditional heartlands. When the club's very existence came under threat, supporters reacted with fury and a fierce determination to defend it to the end. It's a lengthy saga and Tim deals with it in some depth in a chapter called 'The Brighton Stadium Mystery' in a book called *Rebellion: The Growth of Football's Protest Movement*. What follows is a necessarily abbreviated version of events.

Brighton's financial problems began soon after the most successful spell in their playing history. After four seasons in football's top flight, they damn nearly overcame Manchester United in the FA Cup Final of 1983. Gordon Smith, scorer of Albion's first, was through on goal with only keeper Gary Bailey to beat with the score 2–2 deep in the last minute of extra time. 'And Smith must score!' bellowed radio commentator Peter Jones. He didn't, needless to say, and United went on to win the replay 4–0. But Smith lives on in Albion folklore through a fanzine with a title that exactly reproduces Jones's immortal words.

After their moment in the sun, Brighton descended into gloom. They played that final knowing that they were already relegated. Now the club faced the financial consequences of over-spending while trying to keep up with the big boys. By the early 1990s, the tax man was moving in for the kill.

BRIAN CLOUGH'S SHORT STAY AT THE GOLDSTONE GROUND WAS HARDLY HIS FINEST HOUR. HE WAS BROUGHT TO THE CLUB IN 1973, ALONG WITH HIS LONG-TIME ALLY PETER TAYLOR, BY THEN CHAIRMAN MIKE BAMBER, DURING CLOUGH'S TENANCY BRIGHTON LOST 4–0 TO WALTON AND HERSHAM IN THE FA CUP ON A WEDNESDAY AFTERNOON DURING THE THREE-DAY WEEK, AND FOLLOWED UP BY LOSING 8–2 TO BRISTOL ROVERS ON THE SATURDAY. TAYLOR LOOKED ON THE BRIGHT SIDE, POINTING OUT: 'WE WERE THE FIRST TEAM TO SCORE TWO AGAINST ROVERS THAT SEASON.'

PERHAPS THE MOST SUCCESSFUL BRIGHTON MANAGER WAS ANOTHER FORMER SPURS AND ENGLAND MAN, ALAN MULLERY, WHO WON TWO PROMOTIONS IN THREE SEASONS AND TOOK THE CLUB INTO FOOTBALL'S TOP TIER IN 1979. MULLERY WOULD LATER BECOME MANAGER AT CRYSTAL PALACE, THE CLUB THAT BRIGHTON FANS REGARD AS THEIR FIERCEST RIVALS.

He wasn't the only one.

Enter Greg Stanley, then chairman of Focus DIY, and his managing director Bill Archer, a Lancashire man with a home in a village near Blackburn that would eventually witness a peaceful demonstration by Albion fans desperate to save their club. Archer and Stanley brought in enough new money to pay off Brighton's immediate debts – money that had been borrowed from the Co-operative Bank. They also brought in as chief executive one David Bellotti, the former Liberal Democrat MP for Eastbourne, to cut costs to the bone.

'By that time the Taylor Report [into football safety] had been published,' Tim points out, 'and the Goldstone was seen as too small a location for an all-seater ground to be financially viable. The scheme to sell it was presented to fans as increasing the club's borrowing power while efforts were made to secure a new ground elsewhere.' Various locations were mooted, none of them with any hope of success. Then a new plan came to light in the summer of 1995. It was to share Fratton Park with Portsmouth FC, 48 miles away. Supporters were understandably incensed.

The Brighton *Argus* began digging, with the help of accountant and long-time Albion supporter Paul Samrah, who unearthed an explosive nugget of information after scouring the Land Registry. The Goldstone had been sold to property developers Chartwell Land for £7.4 million.

What's more, the club's constitution had been changed. A key clause – stating that, in the event of the club being wound up, any surplus remaining after the settling of debts and the repayment of share capital must be given to a sporting club or charity in Sussex – had been removed. In other words, the club could now be shut down, the debts paid off, the ground turned into a retail park and the shareholders could walk off with a healthy profit from a minimal investment. Archer had bought a majority shareholding for just £56.25.

There followed two years of petitions, demonstrations, protest marches, banner waving, intense lobbying and widespread disruption of matches. The final game of the penultimate season at the Goldstone Ground had to be abandoned after 16 minutes. York City were the visitors, their travel-weary fans looking on with bemusement as the pitch was swamped by home supporters. Both crossbars were broken. 'A riot,' the tabloids dubbed it.

A riot! In Hove! But this was no joke. A handful of hooligans were arrested and sent to prison. Many more peaceful protesters eventually drifted back to the terraces where some onlookers were openly weeping. The ultimate outcome was an eleventh-hour deal with Chartwell who leased back the ground for one more season. To cut a very long story short, Brighton and Hove Albion never did have to play their home games at Portsmouth. They had to travel to Gillingham instead, which was even further away. Fans faced a round

GRAHAM EDWARDS, 60
Chairman of Brighton Hockey Club

'I was first taken to the Goldstone by my grandfather in 1956 when I was four. It would have been a shilling to get in, but Granddad used to lift us over the turnstiles.'

JOHN EDWARDS, 67
Graham's brother and manager of Brighton Hockey Club

'Our mother sold tea and Bovril on the East Terrace and also worked on the turnstile that Granddad used to lift us over. And, yes, he was her father. We used to get there quite early and I'd run down to the front of the East Terrace and stand on an old Tamplins Brewery crate.'

CHRIS PARKER, 66
Publisher

'I'll never forget the game against Watford on a midweek evening in April 1958. We won 6–0 to clinch the old Division Three South. There were over 31,000 rammed into the Goldstone Ground and we boys were allowed on to the cinder track around the pitch. I was right by the corner flag at the North Stand, about four foot from some of the players. Adrian Thorne, a local lad, scored a hat-trick in the first 10 minutes, and added two more either side of half-time. It was phenomenal.'

trip of over 140 miles to watch a home game. It couldn't go on like that, and it didn't. After two seasons in exile, the club came home after intense negotiations between the local authority and the new board, chaired by advertising executive and long-time supporter Dick Knight. The new ground was Withdean Stadium, sited in an upmarket suburb of Brighton and designed for athletics rather than football. 'The seats were the other side of the running track so it was hard to generate much atmosphere,' Tim recalls. 'Still, we won two promotions in a row there, finishing up in the Championship. I think Withdean was a bit of a culture shock to the likes of Derby and Wolves. I remember Derby's Fabrizio Ravanelli coming off the subs' bench to warm up and trying to dodge the long-jump pit.'

Albion stayed at their temporary home for just over a decade. A club that has yo-yoed between the divisions for much of its history was on an upswing. After prolonged wrangling over planning procedures at local and national level, the hugely impressive American Express Community Stadium, otherwise known as The Amex, opened for business at the beginning of the 2011–12 season. The ground stands on the edge of the South Downs, close to Falmer railway station. Before the end of that season, plans were afoot to increase the 22,500 capacity by another 8,000.

By a strange coincidence, Albion's first competitive visitors to the ground were Doncaster Rovers, the club they had beaten 1–0 in that last game at the Goldstone 14 turbulent years previously. Home fans could hardly be blamed for luxuriating in their new surroundings. 'The ironic thing is that if Archer had never been involved, the Goldstone might never have been sold and we wouldn't have ended up with the beautiful ground that we have today,' says Tim before uncoupling his bike from the railings around that ancient chunk of rock and setting off to join the traffic sweeping down the Old Shoreham Road and past the site where so much of his past is forever entombed.

Fans on the pitch after the last ever match at the Goldstone against Doncaster Rovers. April 26th 1997.

HIGHBURY

It was 29 February 1972, and Arsenal were about to play a fifth-round FA Cup replay against Derby County at three o'clock on a Tuesday afternoon. Yes, Tuesday afternoon. Why not Tuesday evening? Because the power workers were on strike and there was no guarantee that the floodlights at Highbury would come on, let alone stay on for 90 or so minutes.

At the time I was living close to the ground and our flat would be regularly plunged into darkness – sometimes because of power cuts and sometimes because we were strapped for five pence to stick in the meter. Just as well that I didn't have to pay to get into that Tuesday afternoon match. Sitting in the press box, I was one of the few people working among the crowd of over 63,000.'

Nick Hornby was there, too. He mentions it on page 59 of *Fever Pitch*, his engaging account of the angst of being addicted to Arsenal long before Arsène Wenger introduced fantasy football to Highbury. Young Nick had bunked off school for the afternoon and was astonished to find himself among the biggest crowd of the season. 'I was disgusted,' he writes, before moving his tongue from one cheek to the other and going on to say: 'No wonder the country was going to the dogs! My truancy prevented me from sharing my disquiet with my mother (an irony that escaped me at the time), but what was going on?'

Not much in football terms, that's for sure. Hornby was spot on when he recalled: 'The replay finished nil-nil, a game with no merit whatsoever.' But, like him, I'll never forget the occasion. I was 23, not too long out of university and evidently considered wet behind the ears by the hardened hacks of the *North London Weekly Herald*. The paper's head office was on Tottenham High Road, so no prizes for guessing which club hogged the back-page headlines. Never mind that the Gunners were not only League champions but also FA Cup holders at the time. To neutrals – and to Spurs fans in particular – they were still 'boring, boring Arsenal'. The most junior member of staff could be safely dispatched to cover the match.

The best part about it was picking up my press pass beforehand. It meant that I was granted access to the marbled halls inside that imposing art deco East Stand. Alas, there wasn't much chance to appreciate Jacob Epstein's bust of Herbert Chapman, the manager who

26TH AUGUST 1933: THE BEGINNING OF THE FOOTBALL SEASON SEES ARSENAL PLAY BIRMINGHAM CITY.

laid the foundations for the great Arsenal side of the 1930s to win five League championships and two FA Cup finals. The engraved tiles were covered with expensive-looking shoes as Crombie overcoats and sheepskin-lined car coats rubbed shoulders in the throng. I remember spotting Malcolm Allison, who was as famous in the 1970s as Chapman was in the 1930s, albeit with fewer trophies to show for it.

Nearly 40 years on and I find myself tentatively pushing at the front door of the marbled halls once more. To my surprise it opens. Some maintenance men have just gone in to work on one of the luxury apartments that now occupy the Grade Two listed East Stand and, while they're keeping the security man busy, I seize the opportunity to take a closer look at Chapman. Cast in bronze, he's staring steadfastly ahead, his stern features bordered by broad lapels, slightly turned up at the ends as though his raincoat had been drying out in front of a coke oven. This time I can see the engravings in the marble tiles around him – here a capital A for Arsenal, framing a leather football; there the cannon that has long been the Gunners' emblem. It's a reminder of the club's origins near Woolwich Arsenal on the south bank of the Thames in 1886. The move north of the river came in 1913. But it was the development of this stunning stand in the 1930s that gave Highbury its unmistakable aura. 'This is the stately home of Arsenal,' it seemed to proclaim, 'and we're a cut above the rest.'

Even the French are impressed. There's a major European game tonight, just up the road at the Emirates Stadium, and, although kick-off is still seven hours away, fans of Olympique de Marseilles are strolling the streets in anticipation. Turning the corner into Avenell Road, they slow down, stand back and gaze upward in awe. Out come the cameras and the mobile phones. They couldn't look more reverential if they were gazing for the first time at Notre Dame or Rouen Cathedral.

Handsome as it is, however, the East Stand is still a façade. It hasn't witnessed football since 7 May 2006, when Thierry Henry scored a hat-trick in a 4–2 win over Wigan. 'For the history of the club and for this building here, to finish on a high I am very proud,' Arsenal's all-time highest scorer told the BBC. And what happened to 'this building here'? It became the site for apartments with price tags that would put them well out of reach of most of the heaving mob that used to stand on the North Bank.

In the marketing suite for what is now Highbury Stadium Square, a young man in a sharp suit tells me that two-bedroom flats are going for half a million, and you can double that for a penthouse. The suite lies just beyond what used to be known as the South Bank, or the Clock End, where I sometimes used to stand on Saturday afternoons in 1972. The football wasn't memorable but some of the comments were. During a game against Liverpool, one of the linesmen pulled a muscle. The cry went out from the public address system: 'Is there

ARSENAL WON THE LEAGUE TITLE WITH A GOAL DIFFERENCE OF 0.099 OVER PRESTON NORTH END IN 1953. BUT THEY WENT OUT OF THE FA CUP IN THE SIXTH ROUND TO BLACKPOOL, WHO WON 2–1 AT HIGHBURY. 'IT WAS MY FIRST GAME AND I REMEMBER STANLEY MATTHEWS MESMERISING OUR DEFENCE,' SAYS DAVE SUTTON, 69, FROM ESSEX ROAD, ISLINGTON. 'I KEPT SHOUTING "GET ON TO HIM", BUT THEY COULDN'T.' THE RESILIENCE OF THE FABLED ARSENAL BACK FOUR WAS STILL SOME WAY IN THE FUTURE.

a linesman in the house?' (or words to that effect). Out of the West Stand strode Jimmy Hill, then analyst of *The Big Match* on London Weekend Television. With the crowd chanting his name deliriously, he quickly changed into a tracksuit and did his duty. Whenever he strayed too close to the touchline, however, a wag behind me would bawl: 'Mind his chin.' Can't remember much about the match but, having checked online, I see that it was another 0–0 draw. There were a lot of those at Highbury that year.

And what can we see from the Clock End now? An 'award-winning' garden where the pitch used to be, created by one Christopher Bradley-Hole. From Chelsea, if you please. Well, he made his name at Chelsea Flower Show. Here he's created a series of squares, the grid pattern apparently designed to reflect the straight lines of the stands.

There's a bit of a breeze this lunchtime and the hedges and ferns begin to sway in unison, just as the crowds once swayed on the North Bank as Arsenal advanced on goal. Tom Watt, the actor, radio pundit and self-confessed Arsenal addict, rates his favourite as the one scored by Ian Wright against Southampton in 1992 after he set off on a mazy 60-yard run from inside his own half and beat four or five defenders. That was the last match before seats replaced the old terracing. For Graham Weaver, author of *12–Nil to the Arsenal*, a treasured memory was Tony Adams scoring the fourth in a 4–0 victory over Everton to clinch the Premiership title in 1998. 'I sat in the upper tier of the North Bank and

that was the afternoon that we realised it actually bounced,' he recalled in BBC Sport's *Highbury Memories*. 'It was a little worrying at the time.'

In the circumstances, the move from Highbury to the Emirates was a no-brainer. The requirement for all-seater stadia that followed the Taylor report of 1989 had reduced the capacity to 38,419. This for a ground that had once hosted a crowd of over 73,000. Hornby recalls paying 25p back in 1973 to stand on the North Bank for a match against Ipswich Town. Twenty years on and spectators were expected to fork out £1,000 to reserve a seat for the season, '*plus the price of a ticket*'. Yet there was no shortage of demand. Indeed there was an extensive waiting list for season tickets. After briefly flirting with the idea of a move to Wembley Stadium, the club set out to build its own arena at Ashburton Grove, confident that all 60,355 seats would be filled.

The Emirates lies within easy walking distance of Highbury. Either side of the Arsenal tube station, stall-holders are already laying out their wares for tonight's match just after 1pm. 'Fat Harry's Foot-long Smoked Hamburgers', proclaims a lengthy sign. Harry himself turns out to be a Greek Cypriot whose father came to these shores in 1957. His real name is Chris Haritakis and he's not particularly fat. Sporting a flat cap with sunglasses dangling from his V-neck jumper, he's happy to leave the stall to his assistants for a moment and reminisce about life on the North Bank. 'I started going when I was a kid in the early 70s,' he recalls,

MARTIN KEMP, 61

Veteran of the North Bank

'At one time it seemed that every half-time drink I bought at Highbury had sugar in it. Even the Bovril...'

and I used to sit on one of those crash barriers. Which was fine until West Ham fans invaded and sent me flying.'

Ah, yes, the good old days of terror on the terraces.

In the late 1980s Harry himself was arrested for running on the pitch when Michael Thomas scored against Spurs. Not that the £75 fine stopped him doing it again, 'somewhat inebriated', some 10 years later. 'It was an end-of-season match with nothing at stake and David Seaman let me put one past him during the warm-up.'

Passing Marseilles fans, weaned on bouillabaisse perhaps, are finding the lure of lunching on a foot-long smoked Frankfurter easy to resist. And I have to decline Harry's kind offer to try one. It might be a little filling for one planning to meet some Arsenal supporters for an early-evening meal in a few hours' time.

They gather at the same Bulgarian-owned restaurant before every evening match, these diehard Gooners from the Deep South – Southend in the case of John Ball, a retired insurance underwriter; Blackheath for his old pal Patrick Freestone, a retired FE college principal. Both grew up much closer to the old ground. 'I went to my first match in 1956,' says John. 'It was a cup tie against Bedford Town and I was one of 55,000. I was standing on a box at the time. My dad had bought me a rattle. When I finally plucked up courage to give it a swing, I walloped the bloke behind me. An egg came up on his forehead.'

Two years later John saw the Gunners take on the Busby Babes. 'The crowd was 64,000 and we were on the South Bank, right in front of the clock,' he says. 'United won 5–4.' It was the last game before the Munich air crash.

Pat was also at that game, having recently become a paying customer at the grand old age of 10. He was living in the Ball's Pond Road in the 1950s and could hear the roar from the ground during every home game. Drawn to floodlit evening matches like moths to a flame, he and his mates got in for nothing – but only for the second half. 'They opened the gates at the East Stand at half-time, so we sneaked in,' he explains. 'Everyone round our way supported Arsenal in those days, although there were a few defectors to Spurs when they won the Double in 1961.'

Paying to get into Highbury for the first time cost him one shilling and sixpence, the equivalent of seven and a half pence. 'Everything was one and six in those days.' And now? 'My seat would be 50 quid on the open market.' But it's a season ticket, of course. Cost him £1,200, including six cup ties. And how does he feel about the Emirates? 'I don't have the emotional attachment that I had to Highbury, but I still feel proud when I approach it.'

There are nods of approval around the table. Among those present are two of John's travelling companions from Southend and Martin Kemp, a bookseller who now lives near Pat in Blackheath. He used to travel even further to Highbury as a kid. 'When I was 11, I'd come from Romford on the 251 bus on my own.' What about your dad? 'He was a Leyton Orient fan, but I'd been to two Arsenal away matches with the milkman's son and we'd beaten Fulham 4–2 and Forest 4–0. I thought "Blimey, this team scores four every game!". Sure enough, my first home game in 1962 was a 4–4 draw with Spurs.'

Martin became a committed North Banker, but those four-goal Gunners had flattered to deceive. As the 1960s wore on, Arsenal entered a barren patch. John was there in May 1966 when just 4,554 turned up for a game against Leeds: the lowest ever League attendance at Highbury. 'It was a nothing end-of-season affair and Liverpool were playing in a big European game, live on the telly,' he says by way of explanation. To cap it all, Arsenal lost 3–0. Cue the end of Billy Wright's reign as boss – further proof, if any were needed, that being a respected England captain doesn't make you a respected manager.

England had a rather important match in the summer of '66, so the appointment as Arsenal manager of a little-known physiotherapist called Bertie Mee hardly set the football world on fire. Five years later the club won the League and Cup double, exactly a decade after their biggest rivals had done the same.

For neutrals the Spurs Double-winners had been a far more attractive side. For Arsenal the flowing football would come later, particularly in the 1990s and 2000s. Discipline and organisation were the hallmarks of that team from the early 1970s. But their ability to grind out results kept the Highbury faithful turning up in some numbers. Even at three o'clock on a Tuesday afternoon.

ARSENAL FANS ARRIVE FOR THE LAST EVER MATCH AT HIGHBURY FOR THE MATCH VERSUS WIGAN ATHLETIC ON 7TH MAY 2006.

HIGHFIELD ROAD

Signet Square could be anywhere in urban England. Satellite dishes cling in clusters to the red-brick frontages of starter homes and 'compact' apartments. Windows framed by white uPVC look out over a communal stretch of grass where a group of Asian kids are playing cricket.

It's good to know that somebody's still running about on that site. The grass very roughly approximates to the turf that once hosted Coventry City's home games. Wedged in at the far edge, next door to a children's playground, is a modest piece of artwork unveiled in June 2012. The size of a tin bath and the shape of a fat fish, it commemorates the club's origins as Singer FC in 1883, with a sewing machine and a motor car among the mouldings on the side. Other significant dates in the club's history are picked out on a metallic frontage with a sky-blue tinge. Sadly, it has already been defaced by graffiti.

It was on 30 April 2005 that the Sky Blues said farewell to Highfield Road with a stunning 6–2 victory over Derby County in front of packed stands. Long-serving defender Marcus Hall, Coventry born and bred, played in that match and recalls: 'Everything seemed to go the way we wanted and the atmosphere was just fantastic. It meant that I left with very mixed emotions. We had a brand new ground to go to, but part of me didn't want to leave the old one.'

The team reconvened later that summer at the Ricoh Arena, a purpose-built stadium on the edge of town with a 32,609 capacity, good enough to be selected as an Olympic venue in the summer of 2012. On one side is a busy six-lane highway, on the other one of the biggest Tesco Extras in the country. The stands at the Ricoh, however, have been packed only for visits by Coldplay, Oasis, Take That and Rod Stewart. Oh yes, and Chelsea for an FA Cup quarter-final in 2009. 'On that day we saw the ground's potential,' Hall reflects. 'But you have to have a successful team to realise that potential week in week out.'

Coventry defied gravity for an incredible 34 years, staying in the top flight from 1967 to 2001. The last match of many a season was a fraught affair, the fans ankle deep in chewed fingernails, ears cocked for news of how fellow relegation battlers were faring. But since finally succumbing to the dreaded drop, the Sky Blues have rarely shown signs of climbing back. Indeed, in May 2012 they went down again to the third tier of English football. Even in the Championship, the Ricoh

'I would have been 15 at the time. I was in my usual spot, on the terrace in front of the Sky Blue stand, when Willie Carr and Ernie Hunt pulled off that spectacular "donkey kick" in 1970. We were playing Everton and leading 2–1 when Coventry were awarded a free kick just in front of me on the edge of the box. Carr pincered the ball between his heels and flicked it up, perhaps more seahorse than donkey, whereupon Hunt stepped forward with extraordinary bandy-legged gait and hit a spectacular dipping volley over the four-man wall and into the top corner. The crowd gasped, then went wild. *Match of the Day* viewers voted it goal of the season. But FIFA subsequently banned the party piece by deeming that the ball should complete a full revolution from an indirect free kick before being walloped into the net.'

was all too often less than half full. Crucially, the club no longer owns its own ground. Between planning the new stadium and moving to it, Coventry lost its Premier League status and the money that went with it. The club sank deeply into debt. Together with a charity known as the Alan Higgs Trust, the local authority stepped in to keep the Ricoh deal alive. One consequence is that revenue from catering and other money-spinning ventures has been going mainly into the coffers of Coventry City Council rather than Coventry City FC. Add to that the £1.2 million annual rent for the privilege of playing there – a longstanding bone of contention between the local authority and the hedge fund that owns the club – and it's no wonder that money to buy quality players is in short supply.

And no wonder nostalgia for Highfield Road is almost palpable in pubs across the city and in the streets around the old ground. Not far from what is now Signet Square stands Swan Lane, where I bump into a man sporting sky blue socks under open-toed sandals. His name is Bill Patterson and he has lived around here since coming to Coventry from Belfast when he was 17 in 1961. 'I bought a season ticket for the Kop End the following season and renewed it every year,' he confides. 'But I stopped going when they moved. There was no need for it. Highfield Road accommodated us very well. It was rarely full, but when it was, the atmosphere was terrific.'

This hankering after the comparatively good old days is a sentiment expressed by other passers-by as I bid farewell to Bill and cut through Mowbray Street to King Richard Street. That's King Richard II, since you ask. According to Shakespeare, Thomas Mowbray, Duke of Norfolk, was due to fight what you might call a grudge joust with Henry Bolingbroke, Duke of Hereford, on nearby Gosford Green when the King intervened and banished them both. It's a reminder that, although these streets are lined with Victorian terraces of the kind common around football grounds, Coventry was a significant medieval city at a time when nearby Birmingham was little more than a village.

In football terms, however, Coventry lacks the weighty heritage of West Midlands clubs such as Aston Villa, West Bromwich Albion and Wolverhampton Wanderers. The City's ultimate glory years were 1967, when Jimmy Hill led them to the promised land of the old First Division, and 1987 when they beat Spurs 3–2 in a thrilling Wembley final and, amid scenes of wild celebration, brought the FA Cup back to Highfield Road.

The road after which the ground was named is on the other side of Signet Square from King Richard Street. On the corner is a house with a sign over the door. 'BEDLAM', it reads. And it must have been bedlam round here on 29 April 1967, when a record crowd of 51,455 packed in for that promotion decider against Wolves. City came back from a 1–0

STUART GARDNER, 39
Engineer

'The game I'll never forget was that 5–4 win in 1990. Brian Clough brought his Forest side to Highfield Road on the back of an unbeaten run of 22 games. Unbelievably, though, we were 4–0 up with 12 minutes of the first half to go. Suddenly Forest woke up and scored three in quick succession with Nigel Clough bagging two of them. At half time their fans were chanting 'Four-three, four-three . . .' at us. After the break they scored again and, unbelievably, it seemed that City were going to blow a four-goal lead. But good old Cyrille [Regis] forced one in and sanity was restored.'

SAM MCNULTY, 52
Songwriter and musician

'It was the last match at Highfield Road and I was with my good mate Steve Edgson. 'Edgehog, as he was known, would always bring a hip flask from which we would take a nip every time Coventry scored. That day we scored six, which meant that we left the old ground in an alcoholic haze that erased some of the memories. Not the feeling, though. Definitely not the feeling.'

deficit with goals from Ernie Machin and Ian Gibson. Both goals were followed by a pitch invasion, at which point the public address system informed the boys ranged around the touchline that the referee would abandon the match if it happened again. When Ronnie Rees added a third, the boys stayed put and Coventry moved up a division.

Among the crowd that day were Bruce Walker, 18 at the time, and Pete Kendall, who was 12 and already a Highfield Road veteran of four years' standing. He was one of those allowed onto the touchline. 'I remember being shepherded through the crowd with other youngsters, right to the front and then through a gate.' Pete shakes his head at the improbability of such a memory and takes another swig of his pint. He is an occupational therapist by trade; Bruce is an academic. We're in their local, three miles across the city from the former ground, and the two pals are enjoying the reminiscences of longstanding fans. Not that they knew each other back in '67.

'I was in the West End [stand] that day,' Bruce recalls. 'Normally I'd have a drink in town with some mates and we'd get to the ground around 2.15. But on this occasion we had to get there two hours before kick-off, and it still took us 20 minutes to push our way across to a decent position behind the goal. There were Wolves fans in there as well, remember. No segregation in those days.' And no fighting either? 'Don't remember any.'

Well, it was the dawn of the Summer of Love. Or perhaps bodies were so tightly wedged together that nobody could raise a fist, even if they felt so inclined. The fighting would come later as the 1960s wore on and the 70s loomed. For the most part, though, matches remained peaceable enough for a character dubbed Soupy Sam to hand out hot cups of half-time tea from the edge of the West End and see them passed back over heads to whoever had shouted their orders from the furthest reaches of the terrace.

The late 1960s were boom years for the club. For that first year in the top flight, the average gate was 34,715. With Villa in the doldrums, those upstarts from Coventry were attracting bigger crowds than any club in the West Midlands. It helped that Jimmy Hill was a maestro of public relations as well as management. Or so it seemed to supporters like Pete and Bruce as they looked on with amusement and bemusement at Hill's pre-match stunts. One day he would drive around the pitch at the wheel of a locally produced Triumph GT6 – a sky blue one, of course. Another time he'd ride round on horseback, clad in hunting pink.

These antics would have seemed absurd if he hadn't produced a winning team and instigated what was known as the Sky Blue Revolution in and around the ground. Until Hill's arrival in 1961, Coventry City were known as the Bantams. He changed the colour of

DAVE LONG, 52
Former Olympic marathon runner

'It was 24 August 1976, and it must have been the first home match of the season at the end of a very hot, dry summer. Manchester United's fans were notorious at the time and, sure enough, they set fire to some bushes and trees at the back of the terracing, at the Kop End. I was 15 at the time and not too far away from them when I caught sight of George Curtis barrelling around the pitch in his blazer and City tie wielding a fire extinguisher. His playing days were over by then, but you still wouldn't want to stand in his way. He leapt over the fence, burst past me and cut a swathe through the United fans. They parted like the Red Sea and George put out the fire. Nobody tried to stop him. Unfortunately, United went on to win the game 2–0.'

the shirts and even came up with the 'Sky Blue Song' (tune courtesy of the 'Eton Boating Song') that diehard fans still chorus raucously to this day. Together with chairman Derrick Robins, Hill set about transforming the facilities. Whereas most football grounds were still stuck in the past, Coventry had become synonymous with the bright new world of the 1960s.

The improvements continued after Hill's shock departure in October 1967 to launch his television career. It helped that Robins ran his own building firm. 'On March 16, 1968, the Main Stand was gutted by fire and with it went the Second Division Championship trophy,' wrote the club's historian Jim Brown on his website in 1999, Highfield Road's centenary. 'The stand was rebuilt almost immediately and was completed in time for the start of the next season, although the first two home games were postponed. The third new stand in four years made Highfield Road arguably the most modern stadium in the land.'

Certainly it marked a change from the make-do-and-mend philosophy of the pre-war and immediate post-war years. Miraculously, only the pitch was holed by three direct hits during the Blitz on Coventry in November 1940. The bombs somehow missed the Kop, otherwise known as the East Terrace, which had been built up using waste concrete from the relaying of the city's tram track in 1922. Unscathed, too, was the roof of the West Terrace, apparently transplanted from Twickenham rugby ground at a cost of £2,200 in 1925. 'It provided cover for 11,000 spectators,' writes Brown, 'and during construction it was found that the pitch fell seven feet from corner to corner, a fault not rectified until 1963.' By then, of course, Hill was already leading his chosen club out of the wilderness.

His second coming was not received with so much enthusiasm by the supporters, alas. Having returned as managing director in 1975, he was chairman in 1981 when Highfield Road briefly became the country's first all-seater stadium. Eight thousand extra seats were installed, reducing the capacity from 36,500 to 20,600. Unfortunately, many of those seats were uncovered, which meant that spectators too often found themselves feeling rather damp in the nether regions. The experiment didn't last long and Hill resigned in 1983.

But nearly 30 years on, as he watched a statue to himself being unveiled at the Ricoh Arena, the old maestro could have argued that he was simply being far-sighted. Again. Since the Hillsborough disaster of 1989, all-seater stadia have become the norm. He may also have pondered, however, why there are so few bums on those seats during Coventry's home games.

The obvious answer is that the club is no longer successful on the field. But there are other factors. Let's quickly pop back to Pete and Bruce, still reminiscing in their local. What they and many other Coventry fans miss about Highfield Road is the 'walk up'. The short stroll from the city centre, in other words, taking in a pint here and there on the way and a pork and stuffing 'batch' (or roll) on the way back.

'The old ground wasn't just a stadium,' muses Bruce. 'It was a location. Players change, managers change, even shirts change. So what is it about supporting a team? It's having a place where you gathered with people who wanted the same outcome as you: a win for the City. Highfield Road was always there. The Ricoh is a fine stadium with better facilities, but when they moved away they took part of my history with them.'

And left a site that could be anywhere in urban England.

A HOUSE WHERE HIGHFIELD ROAD ONCE STOOD.

LEEDS ROAD

Huddersfield Town were to the 1920s what Arsenal were to the 30s, and what Liverpool became in the 1970s and 80s and Manchester United in the 1990s and 2000s. They dominated the decade. OK, they didn't accumulate quite so many trophies as those fabled football clubs from the big cities. But, after winning the FA Cup in 1922, the Town went on to land three League titles in a row.

The man who laid the foundations for this remarkable achievement was Yorkshire-born Herbert Chapman. *The* Herbert Chapman – the one who, in 1925, was lured south to the marbled halls of Highbury. 'It meant that he left just before we won our third championship,' says George Binns, long-time Huddersfield fan and former club secretary. 'The same thing happened at Arsenal. He took them to two titles and then died in 1934 before they won the third.'

'Must have been a hell of a manager,' I suggest with startling perception. 'He was well ahead of his time.'

The same could be said of George. Now 79, he was a pioneer of closed-circuit television to combat football hooliganism and the man who oversaw Huddersfield's move to the stunning McAlpine Stadium, as it was known when it opened for business back in 1994. Today it's the Galpharm Stadium . . . for the time being at least. Sponsors' names come and go but style stays. You've either got it or you haven't. Many of the grounds built since this one have a predictable quality. They're far more comfortable than the often haphazardly assembled terraces and stands that they replaced and, for the most part, they offer better views and more sanitary conditions, albeit at a price. But they tend to look very similar. Like the Amex Stadium in Brighton, this one stands out from the crowd. Perhaps it's no coincidence that, in both cases, the architect took account of the surrounding hills to make the stands undulate with the landscape.

'Banana trusses,' George calls the stands here. 'They're cheaper than cantilever stands and they look better as well.'

11TH APRIL 1930: THE PLAYERS OF HUDDERSFIELD TOWN FOOTBALL TEAM ENJOY SKIPPING AS PART OF A TRAINING ROUTINE AT BUXTON, DERBYSHIRE, IN PREPARATION FOR THEIR FORTHCOMING CUP FINAL MATCH AT WEMBLEY.

MEL BOOTH

Journalist

'I was so keen as a youngster in the 1967–68 season that I'd go to watch the reserves one week and the first team the next. By the time we won the old Second Division in 1969–70, we'd graduated from the Paddock to the East Terrace, and I fondly remember the smiling masses as Jimmy Nicholson and co. paraded the trophy after the concluding 3–1 home win over Watford. The crowd was 27,916, but because of that enormous roof, the atmosphere made it seem as though twice that number were packed in. Mind you, the crowd was over 40,000 for the FA Cup replay against Stoke in 1971. We were quite late arriving and I finished up sitting on the fence at the back of the East Terrace, seeing the action only when it came between the openings in the back wall.'

The Royal Institute of British Architects voted the McAlpine Stadium its building of the year in 1994. The Australian who created it, Rob Sheard, has gone on to design, among others, the Millennium Stadium in Cardiff and the Olympic stadia in Sydney and London. All of which makes comparatively humble Huddersfield's decision to commission him seem remarkably far-sighted – particularly at a time when the other brand new grounds on the football horizon were the rather less inspiring Bescot Stadium, Walsall, and Glanford Park, Scunthorpe.

Like Edith Piaf, George has no regrets nearly 20 years on. 'Don't you feel anything?' I ask him when his Honda Civic pulls up on the site of the old ground, roughly 200 yards away. 'Yes, I just feel pleased that we moved to a decent stadium,' he assures me. This from a man who started watching football at Leeds Road back in 1942, when he was six years old, and had to walk three miles to get here. 'It was war-time, of course, and any professional footballer stationed nearby could turn out for Huddersfield. I remember seeing Raich Carter and Tommy Lawton playing for us.'

The spot where Lawton and a host of more regular Huddersfield centre-forwards kicked off is somewhere on the vast expanse of tarmac surrounded by yet another depressingly familiar collection of retail warehouses. There's a metal disc here somewhere that marks the spot. 'I commissioned it,' George reveals. 'Then I had to recommission it because some fanatical fan with a drill dug it up in the middle of the night.'

Now it's the middle of the day and it could be hiding under anything from a Robin Reliant to a 4x4. George doesn't seem to know where it is. Eventually I leave him playing find-the-disc while I go seeking help from the customer services counter at B&Q. A young man in a black shirt and an orange pinafore comes with me as far as the door, gestures into the middle distance and says: 'See that white van?'

'Which one? There are umpteen white vans out there.'

'Second thoughts,' he reflects. 'It might be under that blue one.'

Eventually I commandeer one of his colleagues and she manages to track it down in a space recently vacated by a BMW. The disc turns out to be a dull silvery colour with a plan of the pitch at the centre, surrounded by the words: 'This plaque marks the centre spot of Huddersfield Town AFC.' It's halfway between the far edge of B&Q and the doorway to Allied Carpets.

Beyond the Allied Carpets end of the retail park lies Leeds Road itself, home of the terrace known as the Cowshed because of the shape of its roof. 'It just looked like a cowshed,' George says by way of explanation. 'Opposite was Dalton Bank, otherwise known as the Open End because it was uncovered. That's where the away supporters were housed. And beyond those houses,' he adds, turning to his left, 'was the gigantic East Stand. That could hold 28,000 in the days when it was all terracing.'

Huddersfield's biggest-ever crowd turned out for a sixth-round FA Cup tie in 1932. Herbert Chapman brought his Arsenal side to town and the Gunners won 1–0 in front of 67,037. 'I was here with over 55,000 against Newcastle in another quarter-final in 1955,' George recalls. 'They were winning 2–1 with four minutes to go when we equalised. They eventually won the replay 2–0 in extra time and went on to win the Cup.'

The following year, a waif-like teenager arrived at Leeds Road from his native Aberdeen. 'You could see he was a youngster with promise,' George reflects. He went on to fulfil it across the Pennines in Manchester. But it was here, on the site of this metal disc, that young Denis Law would stand at the start of every game in the early stages of his career. He was eventually sold, in 1960, to Manchester City for the then astronomical figure of £55,000. Huddersfield used much of the money to install floodlights in 1961. Alas, two of them blew down in a gale the following year.

Apart from Law, George's other 1950s favourites were Harold Hassell and Vic Metcalf, both of whom played for England – only twice in the case of Metcalf, a winger who was unlucky enough to be around at the same time as Matthews and Finney. But he will forever be remembered by Huddersfield fans of a certain age for his partnership with centre-forward Jimmy Glazzard, who scored four times from Metcalf crosses in an 8–2 defeat of Everton here in April 1953.

If that was one of the highlights of the post-war years at Huddersfield, the violent crowd scenes that marred a home game against Leeds some 30 years later was a low point. Anticipating trouble, George had collaborated with the local chief superintendent of police to install an early form of CCTV. 'Things were getting out of hand by that time,' he says. And not just in Huddersfield. Such was the impact of what he had begun at Leeds Road that an invitation was forthcoming to make a presentation to Margaret Thatcher and her advisers in Downing Street on the potential of new technology to combat an old problem.

The 1980s were dark days for football. As well as the Heysel and Hillsborough disasters, 56 people lost their lives when fire swept through a wooden stand at Valley Parade, Bradford. Huddersfield offered Leeds Road to Bradford City to play six 'home' games while the stand was being rebuilt. 'What happened at Bradford really made us focus on finding a new ground for ourselves,' says George, who had already been giving the matter some thought.

The last match at Leeds Road, on 30 April 1994, resulted in a 2–1 victory over Blackpool watched by a 'near capacity' crowd of 16,195. Reverse the first two figures and you'd still be 6,000 short of that record crowd back in 1932. It's a telling reminder that, despite their promotion to the Championship in 2012, Huddersfield's real glory days were so long ago that even almost-octogenarian George wasn't even born at the time.

AN AERIAL VIEW OF LEEDS ROAD IN THE 1930S.

MAINE ROAD

I haven't been in Harry Todd's house much longer than 10 minutes or so when he brings out the champagne. A very large bottle, it must be said. 'They call it a jerry summat or other,' he ventures.

'A jeroboam?'

'That's it.'

And that *is* it. We look at the bottle for a while and take in the label on the side, proclaiming it to have been awarded to the man of the match in an FA Cup tie. Harry didn't win it himself, his playing career having peaked at Stockport County reserves. But he was the steward guarding the tunnel and the home dressing room at Maine Road, and the bottle was casually handed to him one day in March 1996 by the mercurial Georgi Kinkladze, with the words: 'Here, H. You can have this.'

Kinkladze had capped a scintillating performance for Manchester City by beating five Southampton players and then casually chipping Dave Beasant to score what was later deemed to be the second-best goal of the season by *Match of the Day*.

Well, if Harry hasn't popped the cork in over 15 years, he's not going to do it today. Perhaps, it strikes me later, he was holding on to it until City won their first League title in 44 years. I console myself with a warming cup of tea and the thought that the contents may well have lost their sparkle by now – rather like Harry himself since City moved away from Maine Road in 2003 after 80 years at the ground with the largest capacity in England after Wembley Stadium.

Now 77, he worked there for 43 of those years. 'Maine Road was my life,' he says flatly. He did a comparatively short spell at what has been known in bewilderingly quick succession as the City of Manchester Stadium, Eastlands and the Etihad before calling it a day. 'They put me on a door somewhere inside, showing punters the way to one suite or another,' he says. 'It meant that I couldn't get to see the game. Football's not like it was. You can't get near the players now.'

23RD DECEMBER 1967. LEAGUE DIVISION ONE. MANCHESTER CITY 4, STOKE CITY 2. STOKE CITY
GOALKEEPER GORDON BANKS TIPS THE BALL OVER THE BAR DURING THE MATCH AT MAINE ROAD.

BARBARA COWLING, 70
Recycling centre manager

'I grew up a few hundred yards from Maine Road and among the row of shops on the corner of our street was a cobbler's. Two first-team players rented a room above what was really a terraced house with a shop frontage. One was Ray Sambrook, the other Cliff Sear, who'd also played for Wales. It would have been the late 1950s and, at the end of the game, they just walked back to the cobbler's with a few kids following them. They didn't climb into their Jags and head off for some mansion in Cheshire...'

'It would be difficult to get out of our house half an hour or so before a match. There'd just be a constant crowd surging past, most of them in damp macs with flat caps.'

STEVE STEWART, 57
Careers guidance executive

'It's taken a bit of getting used to being a rich club. We were traditionally the poor relations in Manchester. My dad used to say: "As a City fan, son, we live in hope even if we die in despair.'

It was very different back in 1968 when City last won the League before going on to lift the FA Cup the following season. Harry talks fondly of that team, not just as players but as men. 'I used to watch the match from the mouth of the tunnel until 10 minutes before half time, then scoot down to the dressing room to make the tea and cut up the oranges. There were none of those fancy energy drinks in those days.'

He was allowed to sit in on the half-time team talk. 'Malcolm [Allison] usually gave it with Joe [Mercer] chipping in every now and then. They were like a double act. So were Franny [Francis Lee] and Buzzer.' Buzzer? 'Mike Summerbee.' (Summer bee, geddit?) Harry continues: 'They were more like a warm-up act in a comedy club. Buzzer was absolutely ace and Franny was a great lad. No edge to him. He loved to wind up Malcolm, mind you.' And did you get on with Mr Allison, Harry? 'I did. He walked my lad Paul into Wembley in '69. Paul was the club mascot at the time.' He pauses for a moment before adding ruefully: 'He's over 50 now.'

What about Colin Bell?

Colin Bell, it seems, was 'funny but very dry.' And the captain, Tony Book? 'He always went for a fag in the boot room before the game. I've still got a picture of him walking round the pitch with Paul after we won the League. He's resting the trophy on the lad's head.'

Out it comes along with other pictures of happy days. On the sideboard are framed shots of Summerbee with his arm round Harry's wife, Bet, alongside Book tossing up with David Nish of Leicester City before that 1969 final. On a wall is a poster of more recent vintage signed by Shaun Goater, Paul Dickov and Nicky Weaver shortly before the move from Maine Road.

The old ground was a short walk from Harry's house and we've just returned from a visit to the site, propelled by a vicious wind and occasional flurries of almost horizontal Manchester rain. We'd met on the corner of Kippax Street, gateway to the three-tier stand built in the mid-1990s and towering over the surrounding houses. It replaced an expansive terrace which housed a swaying mass of humanity on big match days. It's part of football folklore, here and elsewhere, that children were passed to the front over the heads of adults, and young

ONCE AGAIN THE PRESENCE OF STANLEY MATTHEWS IN THE STOKE CITY SIDE HELPED TO DRAW A RECORD CROWD OF ALMOST 85,000 TO MAINE ROAD IN MARCH 1934. AMONG THE MANCHESTER CITY PLAYERS THAT DAY WAS SOMEONE WHO WOULD LATER MAKE A BIT OF A NAME FOR HIMSELF A FEW MILES AWAY AT OLD TRAFFORD, CHAP BY THE NAME OF MATT BUSBY.

Harry was no exception. 'My dad stayed at the back and used to say, "Wait down there at the end of the match and I'll come and find you."'

Todd senior was a good friend of Frank Swift, the legendary City and England goalkeeper who went on to become the *News of the World*'s football correspondent until he perished in the Munich air crash after covering United's fateful match against Red Star Belgrade. He was 44. 'Swifty used to live round the corner from the ground and drink with my dad in the Parkside,' Harry explains. 'He had the biggest hands I've ever seen. Picked me up once, when I was around eight years old, and lifted me right over his head. One-handed. "Hello, young Toddy," he said. Luckily, he didn't drop me.'

On the way back to Harry's house, we pass the imposing edifice of what was once the Parkside Hotel, meeting point for many a City fan before a home game. After being closed and boarded up for some time, it has now been converted into apartments. There are apartments, too, on the site of the old ground – 'contemporary apartments' alongside 'a superb collection of stylish family homes', according to the developers' blurb on what is now known as The Maine Place.

And Maine Road? A ground that housed a crowd of 84,569 for an FA Cup tie against Stoke City in 1934 had been reduced to around 35,000 seats at the beginning of the new century. Plans to extend the capacity to 45,000 were abandoned when the club was offered the chance to move to the stadium that had hosted the Commonwealth Games of 2002. City managed to lose the last match against Southampton 1–0, making the traditional rendering of 'Blue Moon' sound particularly poignant.

There followed, in the summer of 2003, an auction of remnants from the stadium that lasted for seven hours and raised £100,000 for community projects in Moss Side, that deprived area of inner-city Manchester where a huge football ground had been part of the street scene for as long as locals could remember. Photographer Len Grant recorded the demolition, the auction and the supporters who adorned their homes with everything from signage to sinks that once languished in the gents. The result is an evocative book of colour prints called *Full Time at Maine Road*. 'I've never been a football supporter,' Len confides. 'But I felt like a City fan by the end of that project because I saw how much the club meant to so many people.'

Part of the appeal was being cast in the role of the underdog. Suddenly evolving into the wealthiest club in the world, bankrolled by a billionaire from Abu Dhabi, is a concept totally alien to many City fans' view of themselves. United were always supposed to be the top dogs, the magnet for glamour-seeking supporters from other parts of the country and, indeed, the world. They even drew 83,260, a record for a League game at an English club ground, to Maine Road when they played Arsenal there in 1948 while Old Trafford was still recovering from bomb damage. Twenty years later they stole City's thunder by becoming European champions shortly after the Sky Blues had been crowned champions of England. No wonder the blue half of Manchester relishes their victories over the Reds. Never more so, one imagines, than in the 2011–12 season when they did the double en route to winning the title, snatching it away from their cross-city rivals at the very last minute.

BBC music presenter Mark Radcliffe will have enjoyed that as much as any other Manchester 'Blue'. He still remembers 'as one of the greatest days of my entire life' the derby day when City won 3–1 in November 2002. He particularly delighted in the moment when Goater stole the ball from Gary Neville and fired in from an improbably tight angle. 'It was just so poetic,' he recalls in his introduction to Len Grant's book. 'City had done quite well in a number of derbies but you'd never dream that we could beat United in the last one at Maine Road. When that first goal went in early, I thought maybe we had a chance. And that Gary Neville, Shaun Goater moment: well it's like the Zapruder film of Kennedy being shot. I can still see it now, move for move. And Goater drilling it past Barthez, I couldn't believe it. It was a fantastic match, just amazing.'

The younger Radcliffe had sat or stood in various parts of the ground at different times of his life, including the North Stand, the Main Stand and the Platt Lane end. But he finally settled on the Kippax Stand when it opened and he and Marc Riley (formerly of Manchester post-punk band The Fall, now a fellow BBC 6 Music presenter) were offered tickets. 'City were in the Second Division at the time and they'd got this big new stand with nobody in it, so we almost had a row each,' says Radcliffe. 'It took a while to get used to the height and perhaps there was a lack of atmosphere at the top, but I quite liked the way you could see the pattern of play and the space on the pitch.'

It was very different when City had what Steve Stewart, now 57 and chief executive of a careers guidance company, calls with due reverence

The Team. He means the one with Bell, Lee, Summerbee and the rest of Harry Todd's old mates. While Harry was prowling the mouth of the tunnel, young Steve would be on the packed Kippax terracing with his father, his cousins and a school mate. 'Dad was a market trader in Oldham and we'd all pile into his sky blue van and head for Maine Road,' he remembers. 'When Summerbee took a corner, the crowd would sway forward and then surge back again. After one such surge there was a brief drop in the noise level and a bloke 25 yards in front of us shouted: "Has anybody lost their glasses?" Then someone 25 yards behind us shouted: "Yeah, me." And those spectacles were passed over heads all the way from the front of the terrace towards the back before we heard a cry of "Thanks, mate."'

Nobody waved those specs at the ref, by all accounts.

Emma Taylor from Rochdale remembers the last match in 1994 before the Kippax terrace was turned into a stand. She was there with her mother, Valerie, as usual. And, as usual, they stood in their regular spot, between the halfway line and the North Stand goal. 'It was a 2–2 draw with Chelsea and afterwards it seemed so sad to say goodbye to the old terrace,' Emma muses. 'I had no idea that nine years later we'd be saying goodbye to the entire stadium.'

It has taken her a long time to get over the trauma. 'For every match day in the first season at the new stadium, Mum and I would go to Maine Road first. Living 12 miles away with no car, we always got the train to Manchester then the bus to the ground. We'd get off the 111 and then walk all the way round it. Sounds mad I know, but it felt very cathartic to be there when the old place was coming down. It helped the transition, I suppose.'

It's taken some time, but Emma, 37, is slowly but surely coming to terms with watching some of the world's most expensive players in a state-of-the-art stadium with all mod cons. 'We've been back to the old site only two or three times since the demolition ended and only once in the last 12 months,' she says, adding: 'The crowd seemed louder at Maine Road and the bantering chants between the fans in the Kippax and the North Stand is missing. There's a corporate feel about the new place, I suppose. The atmosphere has been quite poor at times, though it is improving lately. It's hard to explain what's missing. It just *is*.'

Champagne football, it seems, can sometimes lack a little sparkle – rather like the unopened jeroboam in Harry Todd's front room.

11TH MAY 2003. MANCHESTER CITY VERSUS SOUTHAMPTON. A BLUES BROTHERS
TRIBUTE BAND ENTERTAINS THE CROWD AT MAINE ROAD. CITY LOST 1—0.

THE MANOR GROUND

To Oxford, city of dreaming spires and aspiring dreams, home of Oxford University and Oxford United; of Magdalen College (founded in 1458 and still going) and the Manor Ground (opened in 1925, closed in 2001). United's former home is now a private hospital.

We're approaching the entrance as we stroll up Beech Road, past substantial Edwardian semis with expensive cars on the drive. The general affluence of the surroundings here in the suburb of Headington was always a marked contrast with the dilapidated state of the old ground.

Some of the Manor's neighbours must have been glad to see the back of it. Every other Saturday afternoon and some evenings their privacy would be invaded by football supporters from near and far. Not too many, mind you. The capacity was 9,500 by the time closure came and, for the most part, the ground was rarely more than half full. Even during the heady days of the mid to late 1980s, when the club spent three seasons in the top flight, slightly fewer than 14,000 could squeeze in.

The biggest crowds turned up within a few weeks of each other during the winter of 1964, four years after the club had finally been admitted to the Football League and changed its name from Headington United to Oxford.

'We drew Blackburn Rovers in the fifth round of the Cup and they were a top side at the time,' recalls my guide, Dave Sternberg. 'Tickets went on sale at eight o'clock on a Sunday morning and they were already queuing around the block by that time. My dad and I finally got to the window some four hours later. The capacity at the time was around 18,000, but the club built a temporary stand that accommodated another 4,000 or so. And they kept it there after we beat Blackburn 3–1 and drew Preston in the next round.'

Even more turned up for that one, a record crowd of 22,750. Not enough, alas, to will Oxford on to victory. 'We went down 2–0, but both goals were hotly disputed. They kept showing the second goal on *Match of the Day*. It was monstrously offside.' Dave is 61 and a freelance economist by trade. He is one of the few who straddled the line between town and gown – a local lad who went to Hertford College, Oxford, to read Politics, Philosophy and Economics. But he still talks with the passion of one whose footballing allegiance was forged on the terraces of the Manor Ground.

OXFORD UNITED VERSUS BRIGHTON AND HOVE ALBION. THE MATCH ENDS IN A 1—1 DRAW, 10TH FEBRUARY 1996.

'When I was about 10, my brother and I were ball-boys at the Manor Ground. We had to retrieve balls when they ballooned out of the ground – usually on to the bowling green at the Cuckoo Lane end. The bowlers were pretty good about it, as long as we didn't trample on their precious grass.

'We didn't get paid for our work but groundsman Les Bateman, who employed us, allowed us free entry and the chance to sit in the players' dugout. The captain, Ron Atkinson, had legs like tree trunks and before every match he'd rub embrocation into them, which was supposedly good for the muscles. The result was that Big Ron's legs practically glistened. I swear that if you'd squeezed them (God forbid) he'd have shot skyward like a bar of soap. Once he started playing, they'd turn very red. His performances, therefore, were always dazzling though not necessarily because of any great skill on the ball,

The only indication that there was once a football ground here is a sculpture set into a wall near the front entrance of what is now the Manor Hospital. According to a nearby plaque, the artist wanted to link football crowds with the site's current function as a healthcare centre for those who can afford to pay. The sculpture symbolises 'caring and sharing', she suggests. Well, if you say so, madam. While the touchline on the Beech Road side ran in front of what is now the hospital's reception desk, Oxford's most fervent fans gathered at the London Road end of the ground where caring attitudes towards away supporters were somewhat lacking during the 1970s and 80s. Dave cut his teeth there in the more peaceful late 1950s and early 60s, walking to the ground or going on his bike and leaving it in a locked shed behind the Britannia pub. He would have been eight or nine when United stormed up from the Southern League in the 1959–60 season under the captaincy of one Ron Atkinson.

'We called him The Tank,' he recalls. 'He wasn't a particularly skilful player but he was absolutely inspirational as an old-fashioned right-half. If Oxford were 2–0 down, he'd get the ball and just charge with it.

His brother Graham was an inside forward and our all-time top scorer.' That's true, but it took him the best part of 15 seasons to score 107. John Aldridge managed to net 90 in just under three seasons at the Manor Ground, two of them playing at the highest level, before moving on to Liverpool in January 1987.

Another shooting star from Oxford's glory years, Dean Saunders, would eventually move to Anfield as well, but only after first joining Derby in a £1 million deal brokered by chairman Robert Maxwell. United's manager Mark Lawrenson quit soon after it went through and, after a short spell at Peterborough, evidently concluded that he could enjoy a somewhat less stressful and undemanding life as a BBC pundit. Maxwell, meanwhile, could have been a hero at the Manor Ground. The 'bouncing Czech', as Fleet Street dubbed him, had saved the club from bankruptcy in 1983 and it was under his chairmanship that they won promotion to the old First Division two years later and the League Cup the year after that. But in 1987 he bought into Derby County, installed his son Kevin as chairman at Oxford and then bought United's star player.

'To collect for local charities, a blanket was carried around the edge of the pitch so that the crowd could throw in coins. Can you imagine what today's health and safety experts would make of that? Miraculously, perhaps, I was never hit, although sometimes I'd have to carry a corner. At other times my brother and I would have to retrieve coins that missed and throw them back in the blanket. I'm ashamed to say that sometimes the odd penny would end up in our pockets.'

The Maxwell years had already been well and truly soured for the fans by his proposal to merge their club with nearby Reading to form the Thames Valley Royals. The very name sounds more like an ice hockey club or, as the *Oxford Times* drily observed, 'an obsolete Berkshire yeomanry regiment'. Not surprisingly, Reading supporters weren't keen either. As usual with near-neighbours, there was no love lost between the two clubs and mass protests followed at both grounds. In the end, though, it was an upheaval in the Reading boardroom that scuppered the deal.

Maxwell was never one to take much notice of internal opposition, as the following story from Oxford programme editor Martin Brodetsky bears out. 'He once called an AGM at 12 noon when he knew full well that most of the shareholders couldn't make it. Just to make sure they couldn't be there, he started it at five to with the club secretary present and hardly anyone else. Then he marched out to his helicopter, which was parked on the pitch, and, much to the consternation of the groundsman, urinated on the centre circle before taking off.'

United's lengthy search for a new stadium was finally brought to an end by a more recent chairman, Firoz Kassam. It's called the Kassam Stadium and it's sited beyond the ring road and close to Blackbird Leys, one of the biggest public housing estates in Europe. 'The Manor Ground was falling apart and there's no way they could make it all-seater,' Martin says before conceding, 'The new ground does look from the outside as though it was built on the cheap and the west stand was never built at all, so it's open at one end.'

Oxford were relegated in the season that they said goodbye to their old home and slipped out of the League altogether in 2006–7. But they returned to League Two four years later, finishing just two places outside the play-off zone in 2012.

Some cause for optimism then. In seasons to come, the city of dreaming spires and aspiring dreams could once again harbour an aspiring team.

NATIONWIDE LEAGUE DIVISION TWO — OXFORD UNITED VERSUS PORT VALE BALLOONS ARE INFLATED
BEFORE OXFORD UNITED'S LAST EVER LEAGUE MATCH AT THE MANOR GROUND. 1ST MAY 2001.

NINIAN PARK

My taxi driver turns out to be a Leeds United supporter. 'Lived here since I came out of the forces and married a local girl,' he says as we set off from Cardiff Central station. Ten years on and the trauma of what happened here in a pulsating cup tie between Cardiff City and Leeds at Ninian Park has finally faded, although his mates on the cab rank do their best to keep it fresh in his memory. 'Football or rugby: they give me plenty of stick,' he confirms.

For Cardiff fans, that third-round FA Cup tie against Leeds in January 2002 will remain branded into the brain as long as Ninian Park is talked about. 'The atmosphere was like a bear pit,' recalls Steve Tucker, football correspondent of the *South Wales Echo* and a long-time Cardiff supporter. 'Leeds were top of the Premier League at the time and we were 53 places below them. We like to think that we precipitated their decline. I can see Scott Young now hitting the winner in the 86th minute.'

I can see it too, having found it on YouTube. Even filtered through the medium of television, the roar from the crowd gives the impression that it might have been heard in Swansea and quite possibly Llanelli. Cardiff chairman Sam Hammam had left the directors' box and was prowling around behind the goal with the best view in the house when Young's close-range shot hit the net. Up in the Sky commentary box, Andy Gray

confirmed what many of us had long suspected about Ninian Park in general and the Grange End in particular. 'It *is* intimidating, I have to say,' growled the fearless former striker.

Steve felt intimidated, not at all at home on the Grange, when he was first taken there by his stepfather as a small boy in the 1970s. 'It was hooligan central in those days,' he says. 'Heavy boots were stamping up and down on wooden slats. Looking back now, it seemed to me like Dante's Inferno. I wondered why my stepdad had brought me to this terrible place.'

As he grew up, however, he would go back again and again with his mates. 'There are times now when I wish we were back at Ninian Park,' he muses. 'But only when I remember the good times. Some seasons were pure tedium. By the end of the 1995–96 season, I think it was,

1ST DECEMBER 1945: DYNAMO MOSCOW GOALKEEPER KHOMICH KICKS THE BALL UP FIELD AT
CARDIFF CITY'S NINIAN PARK GROUND DURING HIS TEAM'S BRITISH TOUR. CARDIFF LOST 10–1.

THE LAST SEASON AT NINIAN PARK WAS 2008–9 AND THE LAST MATCH WAS LOST – 3–0 TO IPSWICH TOWN UNDER THEIR NEW MANAGER, ROY KEANE. HAD CARDIFF NOT BEEN MOVING TO THEIR SPANKING NEW STADIUM, THE TWO STANDING AREAS WOULD HAVE BEEN CLOSED DOWN AND THE CAPACITY REDUCED TO JUST 13,000.

we'd managed to clock up no fewer than 23 draws and finished fourth from bottom of the fourth tier. There wasn't even a re-election fight to make it interesting.'

For the time being at least, the new ground is named after the club rather than a sponsor.

The Yorkshire cabbie drops me outside the Cardiff City Stadium in a car park the size of Barry Island with the usual retail warehouses ranged around us, including the obligatory drive-thru' McDonald's and KFC. The stadium looks much the same as most other new grounds, except for the Welsh signage. Club historian and former Radio Wales commentator Richard Shepherd gives me a guided tour, including a glimpse into the home dressing room where 'Carpe Diem' is emblazoned on a wall with the Welsh equivalent alongside it. 'I don't

think too many of our squad can speak Welsh,' Richard confides. Nor Latin, I dare say, yet nowhere can I see the words 'Seize the day'.

The site of Ninian Park is a short walk away, a hundred yards or so behind the Ninian Stand. To get there you cross a vast expanse of tarmac, at the far end of which some bricks are embedded. Close up you can see that they're engraved with supporters' names and messages. They form a pathway to the old gates which have been re-hung on the former portico, thus providing a suitably dignified portal to the past. Only an empty burger box impaled on some nearby railings lowers the tone somewhat.

Beyond the gates and across the main Sloper Road, the former pitch is buried somewhere under a rather Scandinavian-looking development of new housing. In there, too, and silenced for good is the former

Grange End. Alongside it was what used to be known as the 'Bob End'. Between 1919 and 1939 you could get in for a shilling.

The cul-de-sac nearest to us is called Barclay Wilson Close, named after the founder of the club. 'He ran the Riverside Cricket Club and wanted to keep the players together during the winter months,' Richard explains. 'Back in 1910, he found this site and built a football ground on what had previously been allotments and a rubbish tip.'

So why isn't it called Wilson Park, or even Barclay Park? Because Cardiff Corporation apparently needed financial guarantors and one of them was the son of the frightfully important third Marquess of Bute, one Lieutenant-Colonel Lord Ninian Crichton-Stuart. Ninian Park it was then.

The old ground was not just the home of Cardiff City; it was also where the Welsh national side played. In fact, the record crowd was 62,634 for a match against England in October 1959. 'The club record of nearly 58,000 turned out to watch City take on Arsenal in April 1953,' says Richard, who was taken to his first match by his father, aged 11, just three years later. 'Against Portsmouth it was. Trevor Ford played, and so did Gerry Hitchens.'

Ah, now you're talking. My dad used to watch Ford at Villa Park in the late 1940s, and we both watched Hitchens in the early 60s. He was my boyhood hero, hitting 41 goals in the 1960–61 season. But that's enough about Villa Park. 'What about Ninian Park?' I hear you say. 'Over to you, Richard,' as they used to say at Radio Wales: 'Ford was loved by the fans here, but not by the directors. His attitude was that if he could pull in crowds of forty, fifty or even sixty thousand, as he had at Villa,

CARDIFF CITY'S MOST SUCCESSFUL YEARS WERE IN THE 1920s. THEY MISSED OUT ON BEING CROWNED LEAGUE CHAMPIONS BY GOAL DIFFERENCE TO HUDDERSFIELD TOWN IN 1923–24. BUT AT LEAST THEY WON THE FA CUP THREE YEARS LATER BY BEATING ARSENAL ON ST GEORGE'S DAY, 1927. WHEN IT CAME BACK TO NINIAN PARK, IT WAS THE FIRST TIME THAT THE CUP HAD BEEN 'LET OUT OF ENGLAND', AS COMMENTATORS SAID AT THE TIME. MANY YEARS LATER THE COVETED SILVERWARE WOULD BECOME A REGULAR VISITOR TO WALES AS THE MILLENNIUM STADIUM, CARDIFF, HOSTED THE FINAL WHILE WEMBLEY WAS BEING REBUILT.

then he should be paid accordingly. On one occasion, he refused to play simply because the manager wanted him at inside right and Hitchens at centre forward. The directors suspended him for two weeks on no pay, but he made up his wages by selling his story to the *Sunday Empire News*.'

And Hitchens?

'He signed for Villa in 1957 and came back to Ninian Park with them on Easter Saturday, 1960. We were vying with them for the Second Division championship, both clubs having pulled away from the pack with a few weeks to go. Hitchens must have been injured because he didn't play that day. But I was in the enclosure in front of the Main Stand and I remember him being cheered all the way to the visitors' dugout by the home fans. There was less animosity in those days.

'Anyway, Graham Moore scored the only goal of the game and Cardiff seemed odds-on to win the title. Three days later we played Plymouth at home, and they were in the relegation zone. We hadn't had a penalty all season, but we had two in this game and missed them both. Brian Walsh put the first one past the post at the Canton End. Danny

Malloy took the second and hit the goalie's chest so hard that the ball rebounded almost to the halfway line. We lost 1–0 and, as a result, missed out on the title by one point.'

'Still, you *were* promoted,' I point out.

'Yes, but we came down again in 1962,' Richard reflects ruefully. 'It's 50 years since we were last in the top flight.' How fitting it would have been had they won promotion half a century on, but in 2012 they lost out in the play-offs yet again.

At least the Welsh Cup gave the club plenty of opportunities to compete in Europe – never more memorably than that mad March night in 1971 when the Bluebirds soared over Real Madrid, beating them 1–0 with a goal from Brian Clark. Richard was there as usual with a crowd of over 47,500. 'I knew it wouldn't be enough and we duly lost the second leg 2–0, but for a while we felt like Kings of Europe.'

Feelings like that have to be savoured. Just ask anyone from Cardiff who was there for that Leeds game in 2002 – apart, that is, from a certain taxi driver.

25TH APRIL 2009 – CARDIFF CITY VERSUS IPSWICH TOWN, COCA COLA CHAMPIONSHIP –
FANS HOLD A FAREWELL BANNER AT THE END OF THE FINAL LEAGUE MATCH AT NINIAN PARK.

NINIAN PARK | 127

PLOUGH LANE

Plough Lane has an agricultural ring to it. With a name like that, it should be a dung-splattered track at the back end of some idyllic village rather than a busy thoroughfare through south-west London. Football fans of a certain age, however, will instantly recognise it as the home of Wimbledon FC until the early 1990s when the club felt obliged to decamp to Selhurst Park, home of Crystal Palace.

Eventually, those who ran Wimbledon made the extraordinary decision to move even further away from their roots and finished up in Milton Keynes. But don't mention MK Dons to those few, those happy few who set up AFC Wimbledon to keep alive the heart and soul of a club whose rapid ascent from the Southern League to the upper reaches of the top flight and an FA Cup Final victory at Wembley was one of the miracles of recent football history.

The mere mention of Plough Lane takes me back 20 years. I'm watching *Match of the Day* with growing incredulity as Dalian Atkinson of Aston Villa sets off on a mazy run from his own half, weaving effortlessly through Wimbledon's normally robust midfield and defence until he reaches the edge of the area and chips over Hans Segers into the net.

Atkinson's effort was voted goal of the season by *MOTD* viewers.

I remember Atkinson's strike partner Dean Saunders leaping on his back and holding aloft an open umbrella borrowed from one of the Villa fans. Yes, it was raining. Again. That bleak, uncovered terrace where away supporters were housed must have been a bit of a culture shock for those more used to the Holte End at Villa Park.

But mention Plough Lane to visiting supporters from any club and they will invariably hone in on the weather. A pal of mine, who follows Coventry, remembers being so wet through that his matches became damp and he was unable to light his pipe. (Yes, the aroma of Old Holborn was not confined to the *Test Match Special* commentary box.) 'I remember going to the Portakabin they laid on as the gents,' he recalls, 'and there was a bloke taking shelter in there and seemingly bent on watching the rest of the match through one of those slit windows.' Were you tempted to join him? 'No, it was too smelly.

TOP: PLOUGH LANE 20TH APRIL 1982.
BOTTOM: WIMBLEDON FANS WITH THEIR MASCOT.

PLOUGH LANE | 129

And just as well. Some time later I noticed that he was being escorted away by the police.'

Another friend, a long-time Brighton fan, was on the away terrace one freezing New Year's Day when the weather turned even more inclement. 'The ball disappeared from view for at least half the game,' he says. 'Wimbledon's habit of booting it way up in the air meant that it vanished into falling snow and low cloud.'

Luckily it's only threatening to snow on the bitterly cold day that I meet up with author, *Guardian* columnist and Wimbledon follower David McKie. We set off from the station past the Centre Court Shopping Centre, the very name a reminder that this neck of the woods is better known for tennis than football.

It's a fair old hike from here to Plough Lane. On the way we pass the town hall, outside which goalkeeper Dave Beasant addressed the throng shortly after captaining the side that turned over Liverpool 1–0 in the 1988 Cup Final. Some 37,000 Wimbledon fans had materialised at Wembley and a fair number of them were here to welcome the team home. Voice laden with irony, Beasant told them that he hoped to see them all at the next home game.

Some chance. Gates at Plough Lane tended to be measured in four rather than five figures and home supporters were regularly outnumbered by away fans during their heady days in the old First Division. 'I think the club expected more support when they were doing well in the top flight,' says David. 'But, if the kids at my children's school were anything to go by, they'd already formed attachments to Chelsea or, to a lesser extent, Fulham.'

His own son could easily have been one of them. 'I took him to Chelsea when he was seven or eight and there was a bit of a punch-up, which frightened him. "Tell you what," I said. "We'll go to non-league Wimbledon. There won't be any trouble there." It was 23 November 1974,' he adds, having written the date on the back of his hand as it might be inscribed on his heart. 'We beat Bath City 1–0 with a goal from a venomous shot by Mick Mahon.'

It was the beginning of a relationship that would see the McKies follow the Dons to this day, albeit not to Milton Keynes. David once wrote a short piece for the *Guardian* leader column under the headline 'In praise of AFC Wimbledon' and admits to feeling a quiet satisfaction at the news of any defeat for MK Dons. He won't be alone there. Many former Plough Lane stalwarts must feel the same. But was he right in promising his son that there'd be no trouble at the old ground?

IN FEBRUARY 1980, MICHAEL FOOT MP VISITED WIMBLEDON TO WATCH HIS BELOVED PLYMOUTH ARGYLE AS A GUEST OF WIMBLEDON FAN AND FELLOW LABOUR POLITICIAN RICHARD FAULKNER (NOW BARON FAULKNER OF WORCESTER). WIMBLEDON WON 3–1, BUT THE SCORE COULD HAVE BEEN A LOT MORE EMPHATIC, ACCORDING TO DAVID MCKIE WHO WAS THEN WRITING ON POLITICS FOR THE GUARDIAN. 'WE PULVERISED ARGYLE,' HE RECALLS. 'WE'D ARRANGED WITH OUR VARIOUS WIVES TO MEET AFTER THE MATCH FOR DINNER AT THE LEMON TREE IN WIMBLEDON VILLAGE, AND WE'D PROMISED THEM: "YOU'LL REALLY ENJOY IT BECAUSE MICHAEL'S THE MOST TERRIFIC TALKER."

'WELL, WE ALL SAT DOWN AND HE HARDLY SAID A WORD FOR THE FIRST HALF HOUR. HE WAS IN A REAL STATE OF DEJECTION BECAUSE HIS SIDE HAD BEEN SO WELL BEATEN. BUT AS THAT FEELING ABATED, HE BEGAN TO TALK MELLIFLUOUSLY AND ENTERTAININGLY ABOUT A RANGE OF SUBJECTS AND BECAME THE LIFE AND SOUL OF THE PARTY.'

EIGHT MONTHS LATER FOOT BECAME LEADER OF THE LABOUR PARTY AND, 30 YEARS AFTER THAT, A PLYMOUTH SCARF WAS DRAPED OVER HIS COFFIN AT HIS FUNERAL IN GOLDERS GREEN.

'I never saw any serious disturbances there.'

Not off the field anyway. That formidable side of the late 1980s were known as the 'Crazy Gang', but they couldn't have been much fun to play against. 'Dennis Wise was devious, niggly but a talented player,' David reminds me, 'and John Fashanu used his elbows to good effect. He terrified defenders.'

Vinnie Jones had a similar effect on opposing forwards. A former hod-carrier who joined the club from Wealdstone FC, he was what you might call a holding midfield player. Certainly few of us will forget the picture of him holding Paul Gascoigne firmly by the testicles. No man can look at that photo without wincing.

We trudge on past rows of substantial Victorian and Edwardian villas – just what you might expect in an affluent part of south London. But as we near Plough Lane itself, it's noticeable that surroundings are

becoming somewhat dowdy. It must have seemed dowdier still after the move to Selhurst. An already run-down ground was used for reserve team fixtures for a while, then abandoned and left to rot until 2002. 'The expectation was always that it would be a Safeway supermarket,' David explains. 'But they couldn't get planning permission. Although the people who live around here weren't sad to see the back of the football ground, they didn't want a Safeway either because of the increased traffic it would bring. So the old place just stood there, going from bad to worse. It was a sad sight to see a ground where you'd had so much entertainment over the years just disintegrating. Wimbledon were very uneasy tenants of Selhurst Park and there were endless negotiations to get us a ground close to our old home. At one point there was talk of us being rehoused in a disused sewage works. Then it was going to be the dog track, but that all came to nothing.'

Sam Hammam, the Lebanese chairman who had overseen Wimbledon's rise and fostered the Crazy Gang image – he once offered to buy Dean

Holdsworth a camel if he scored 20 goals in a season – sold the club to two Norwegian businessmen in 1997. It was they who appointed Charles Koppel as chairman in 2001, and he who pushed through the relocation of the old club to a new town 56 miles away. Luckily, AFC are a little closer. In fact, they're just down the road in Kingston-on-Thames, at what used to be the King's Meadow. It now goes under the rather less bucolic name of the Cherry Red Records Stadium.

And Plough Lane? Well, that is now the Reynolds Gate development, an apartment complex named after Eddie Reynolds, Wimbledon's all-time top scorer. He put away an astonishing 340 goals in 329 matches between 1957 and 1966 when they were a non-league side. Other former players and officials are remembered here as well. Cork House is named after Alan Cork who played for Wimbledon for 14 seasons, appearing in all four divisions of the Football League. And here's Bassett House. Dave Bassett played for the club in the 1970s, but he'll always be better remembered as the manager who took Wimbledon from the Fourth to the First Division during the 80s. Lawrie Sanchez will be remembered too. After all, he scored the winner in that Cup Final. Perhaps that's why his block is on matey first-name terms: Lawrie House.

There's no sign of a Vinnie View or a Fashanu Mews, but they could be in there somewhere. Certainly the whole complex is considerably more upmarket than its surroundings and the ground it replaced – which was little better than 'a slum', according to David, though he adds, 'It was lousy, but it was ours.'

He used to stand on the terrace in front of the North Stand, where the wordsmith in him was intrigued by a fellow fan describing an incoming player from Fulham as having 'puddingy' feet. Or he'd sometimes sit with his son in the South Stand, bought second hand in 1923 from Clapton Orient before they changed their name and location to Leyton. 'On two occasions the stand had to be shut for safety reasons. The floor was made up of wooden slats and litter tended to gather in its grooves. If anyone had dropped a match, it would have gone up in flames.'

The club became more acutely aware of the threat after the Bradford City fire of 1985. But it was, of course, the requirements of the Taylor Report following the Hillsborough disaster three years later that drew down the final curtain on Plough Lane. Long gone now is that bleak away terrace. Gone, too, the somewhat seedy Sportsman pub at the Durnsford Road end and the nightclub that materialised for a while somewhere under the North Stand.

Still flowing, or at least sludging along at the back of what used to be the terrace opposite Durnsford Road is the River Wandle. Yes, Wandle, not Womble. I know we're in Wimbledon but this part feels a hell of a long way from the Common. The river bank is strewn with litter. To the left the skyline is dominated by electricity pylons, to the right are scrubby allotments, and ahead are some of those corrugated plastic warehouses that are found on industrial estates all over the western world.

As you may have gathered, Plough Lane was never as idyllic as it sounded.

WIMBLEDON'S FINAL FIRST TEAM MATCH AT PLOUGH LANE CAME ON 4 MAY 1991, IRONICALLY AGAINST NEW LANDLORDS CRYSTAL PALACE. 10,002 SPECTATORS SAW CRYSTAL PALACE BEAT WIMBLEDON 3-0. MARK WRIGHT SCORES A HAT-TRICK IN 18 MINUTES.

ROKER PARK

Richie Morgan was six when he was first surreptitiously ushered into Roker Park half a century ago. For a while, he never saw much of the turnstiles at the Fulwell End. 'My dad had a very long overcoat and I was usually wrapped inside it so he didn't have to pay for me,' he recalls, adding by way of explanation, 'He was a joiner on the shipyards and they were always in and out of work.'

There was also room in that capacious coat for a home-made swing. Once young Richie was safely smuggled in, he had a better view than most. 'We used to get there early, about one thirty, and Dad would go straight down the front and loop the swing ropes onto the fence. Quite a few other fathers did the same for their kids. We just hung there only a yard or two from the edge of the pitch.

'The thing that really impressed me was the peanut seller. He'd walk round the track and someone halfway up a steep terrace would shout "Peanuts". The money would be passed down to the front and the guy would wrap some up in greaseproof paper and hurl them. Tell you what: he very rarely missed his target. Bet he was a good darts player.'

But what about the footballers, Richie? Who was your favourite? 'It would be Charlie Hurley in those days. He looked like a giant to me, barrel-chested, like Dave Mackay, and a fantastic player. When we won a corner, the crowd would chant his name and up he'd come. He scored some great goals, mostly with his head.' Forty-three of them, to be precise, between his first in 1960 and his departure for Bolton Wanderers in 1969. Not bad for a centre-half.

Hurley had made an inauspicious start to his Sunderland career, scoring an own goal in a 7–0 thrashing by Blackpool in 1957. When that was quickly followed by a 6–0 defeat by Burnley, questions were being asked about this newcomer from the south. (No, not Middlesbrough but Millwall, as it happens – the Deep South, in other words.) Hurley soon won over the crowd, not only with his headed goals but also his ability to bring the ball out of defence and set up attacks. So much so that, three decades after his heyday, he was voted Sunderland's Player of the Century and given the honour of digging up the centre spot after

9TH SEPTEMBER 1961. LEAGUE DIVISION TWO. ROKER PARK, ENGLAND. SUNDERLAND VERSUS LEEDS UNITED. SUNDERLAND
CENTRE FORWARD BRIAN CLOUGH SHOOTS FOR GOAL AS THE LEEDS UNITED GOALKEEPER ALAN HUMPHREYS ATTEMPTS A SAVE.

RON DAVIDSON NOT ONLY PAINTED PUB SIGNS FOR VAUX BREWERY, HE ALSO CREATED AN OFFICIAL CHRISTMAS CARD FOR SUNDERLAND FC. 'I DID AN OIL PAINTING OF THE GROUND CALLED *FAREWELL TO ROKER PARK*,' HE RECALLS, 'AND TOOK IT INTO THE CLUB ONE DAY. BOB MURRAY, THE CHAIRMAN AT THE TIME, JUST HAPPENED TO BE IN RECEPTION. HE TOOK ONE LOOK AND ASKED IF HE COULD BUY IT. I WAS DELIGHTED.'

the last ever game at Roker Park in 1997. It was later transferred to the pitch at the brand new Stadium of Light.

That little ceremony brought to an end almost a century of football at one of the most fiercely partisan grounds in the country. Back in March 1933, it had attracted a crowd of 75,118 for a sixth-round FA Cup replay against Derby County. But the legal requirement for all-seater stadia had reduced the capacity to under a third of that as the 21st century loomed. Put that in the context of the 25,000-seat stadium – rarely more than a fifth full – bequeathed to little Darlington by former safe-blower George Reynolds. Demand at Roker Park was considerably higher and space to expand was non-existent.

Something similar had happened at the end of the 19th century. Roker Park had opened for business on 10 September 1898, with a 1–0 Sunderland victory over Liverpool. The official opening was performed with a gold key in a locked gate by one Charles Vane-Tempest-Stewart. He not only had the longest name in Sunderland but was also the sixth Marquis of Londonderry and president of a club that already had three League titles under its belt. No wonder there was an urgent need to expand from the confines of its former home on Newcastle Road.

It's fair to say that Sunderland enjoyed considerably more success before the Second World War than afterwards. True, they won the FA Cup and the hearts of all neutrals in 1973 by beating Don Revie's formidable Leeds United and emptying the town centre on a Saturday afternoon more effectively than a nuclear alert. There were memorable scenes when the open-topped bus carrying the team and the Cup finally made it through thronged streets to Roker Park. But '73 was a rare achievement compared to '37, when Sunderland triumphed in the final, 3–1 over Preston North End, just over a year after landing their sixth League title.

The club was briefly known as the 'Bank of England' in the early 1950s after splashing out what was considered big money at the time on the likes of Len Shackleton and Trevor Ford. By 1958, however, relegation loomed for the first time. And by no means the last. They even managed to get themselves relegated in that final season at Roker Park, despite beating Everton 3–0 in the last competitive game there.

Not surprisingly, there is no Relegation Avenue among the football-inspired names on the housing estate that now stands on the old ground. There's Midfield Drive, a Turnstile Mews (not as posh as it sounds) and, yes, a Promotion Close. We're standing opposite the sign now, Richie and me. Seagulls swoop over satellite dishes and soar over the children's playground as he scratches his head and ponders where the centre circle might have been.

What's more certain is that the Roker End backed onto the entrance to the estate, across the road from a shop that still calls itself Roker Park News and Booze. 'The Roker End was where the away fans stood, uncovered,' Richie recalls. 'We didn't want to make them too comfortable,' he adds with a grin.

At this point we're joined by long-time season-ticket holder Martin Johnson, who first came here with his father in the late 1960s. 'I'd be eight or nine at the time. All I remember about the match is that we played Arsenal and lost 1–0 to a goal by Ian Ure. But I'll never forget the noise. We stood in the paddock in front of the Clock Stand and there were two great banks either side of us. They generated a stonking atmosphere, very loud and very vibrant. The boisterous fans would get in between two and half past and the singing and chanting would start, building up and building up towards kick-off. These days the new ground has far superior facilities, but much of the crowd don't take their seats until five to three.'

MOST PEOPLE KNOW THAT JAMES HERRIOT WAS A VET WHO WROTE BEST-SELLING BOOKS. MANY KNOW THAT HIS REAL NAME WAS ALF WIGHT, THAT HE GREW UP IN GLASGOW AND TRAINED AT ITS VETERINARY SCHOOL. BUT FEW KNOW THAT HE WAS BORN AND SPENT THE FIRST THREE WEEKS OF HIS LIFE IN SUNDERLAND AND REMAINED A LIFELONG SUPPORTER OF ITS FOOTBALL CLUB. AS HIS WORKLOAD DECREASED TOWARDS THE END OF HIS LIFE, HE SPENT MORE AND MORE SATURDAY AFTERNOONS AT ROKER PARK AND, IN 1992, HE WAS MADE A LIFE PRESIDENT OF SUNDERLAND FC.

'The other thing that struck me when I first went to Roker Park was how beautiful the pitch looked. The turf was superb. During night matches it seemed to shine under the floodlights. There was something about night games. The crowd seemed even louder somehow.'

For the residents of the more traditional red-brick Victorian terraces on the other side of the ground from the new estate – particularly for those in Sandringham Street, hard up against the back of the old Fulwell End – midweek evenings and Saturday afternoons must seem a lot quieter since Roker Park's closure. 'I used to cut through to this street from my grandma's house whenever I could get to a home game and it would be jam-packed with people,' Martin recalls. Unlike Richie, he wasn't born and bred near Roker Park. He grew up in Coventry, albeit the son of Sunderland parents. 'Mum was even more of a fan than Dad,' he says. 'She was brought up in Fulwell, a mile or two from the ground, and her father used to work on the turnstiles.' So why didn't she go and stand on the terraces with her husband and son? 'She was only four foot eleven.' Perhaps she could have done with one of those pitch-side swings.

Martin moved to the North East in 1978 when he secured a place at Newcastle University. He now works on Wearside as an accountant and spends every home match here, as he has for the past 34 years. But he lives on Tyneside, which must lead to some lively conversations with his neighbours. 'There's a lot of leg-pulling,' he concedes. 'Mind you, there are some estates in Newcastle where I'd never come out as a Mackem.'

The term is a legacy of the rivalry between the two near-neighbours. In the days when the riversides of both towns were alive with the clatter of hard work, ships were built on the Wear and fitted out on the Tyne. 'We mack 'em and you tack 'em,' as they said on Wearside. Or 'They mack 'em and we tack 'em,' as the Geordies would put it.

Richie and Martin have fond memories of local boy Gary Rowell, who scored a hat-trick in a 4–1 victory over Newcastle in 1979. The goals were posted on YouTube in 2011 under the heading 'Gary Rowell hat-trick against the Scum'. Well over 34,000 have viewed it, which gives some idea of the animosity between the clubs. 'There's a T-shirt in the club shop,' Richie confides, 'with the message: "I'm not biased against Newcastle. I don't care who beats 'em."'

There has always been a keen rivalry between the two clubs, but only in the past 40 years or so has it become quite so intense and vitriolic. 'It wasn't like that when I was younger,' says retired artist and picture-framer Ron Davidson. 'I used to go to Roker Park one week and St James's the next.' But you were always a committed Sunderland man? 'Oh, yes.'

Maybe people who'd lived through the Second World War had endured the sort of life experiences that put football rivalries into some perspective. Certainly Len Shackleton wasn't demonised when he made the short journey from St James's to Roker in 1948 for a transfer fee of £20,050. Not by Sunderland fans anyway. 'We loved him,' Ron assures me. 'Even if one or two were infuriated by his habit of putting his foot on the ball and taking the micky out of defenders.'

Not for nothing was Shackleton known as the Clown Prince of Football. Ron remembers: 'Long after he'd retired, he came into our shop and bought some paints to have a go at art. I called him "Mr Shackleton" and he said: "I used to be known as Len Shack two stone ago." To which I replied: "I bet you can still play a bit." Then he did his famous trick.' What was that? 'He took out a 50p piece, dropped it on to his shoe and then flicked it straight into his top pocket.'

Len Shack, an outrageously gifted inside left, scored 101 goals in 348 appearances for Sunderland. Brian Clough scored 54 in 61 – almost a

HARRY PEARSON
Guardian, Friday 2 December 2011

'The captain of Sunderland during the club's last truly successful era was Raich Carter. Carter was a tough man, as anyone who grew up in a Durham pit village with the name Horatio would be. Recalling the crowds at Roker Park during the 1930s, however, he softened. "They sacrificed so much to come and see us," he told an interviewer later in his life. "We were their only hope" – and the tears rolled down his cheeks.'

JIM CRAIGS, 80
Former railway guard

'I remember getting to a home game against Newcastle well before kick-off and still being locked out. Apparently there were over 68,000 inside. It was the early 1950s and Len Shackleton was playing for us. What an entertainer he was! The bloke standing next to me at the Roker End one day was right when he remarked that he should be treading the boards at the [Sunderland] Empire. That game was against Arsenal and the defence seemed to stand off him as he dribbled through. I think they were worried about being made to look fools. Anyway, Shack just stood there for a while with his foot on the ball before tapping it in.'

goal a game. After signing from his home-town club, Middlesbrough, in 1961, his career was cut brutally short on Boxing Day the following year after a collision with Bury goalkeeper Chris Harker. Ron was standing at the Fulwell End at the time. 'I can still visualise them colliding,' he says. 'It was awful. Brian was an old-fashioned centre forward. He didn't tackle back, but he could turn defenders rapidly and snatch goals from nothing. I was one of 10,000 who turned out to watch his comeback against Halifax Town reserves. We scored seven that day and Cloughie bagged five of them.'

Cruciate ligament damage in those days, however, made it difficult to sustain a career. After three games back in the first team, Clough called it a day. He was 29. After a spell as youth team coach, he left to manage Hartlepool in 1965, en route to Derby and even greater glory at Nottingham Forest. No wonder Sunderland fans of a certain age still talk about him as the greatest manager they never had.

Before dropping me off near Sunderland station, Richie Morgan's car makes a detour via the Stadium of Light. Nearby burns a monument shaped like a Davy lamp. It's dedicated to the miners who lived and died in this area when this site was the Wearside Colliery. The pits have long gone. So have the shipyards where Richie's dad worked when work was available.

The white metalwork protruding over the walls of the stadium is dazzling in a winter sun that also gleams on a curve in the River Wear. On the opposite bank is the site of the former Vaux Brewery, a local institution and Sunderland FC's sponsor for many years. It was a perfectly profitable business, but not profitable enough for incoming City whizz-kids seeking a better deal for shareholders. They closed it down, putting 550 people out of work. That was over 13 years ago, since when a patch of wasteland has mutated into a temporary car park. 'All we seem to have now,' Richie reflects, 'is a Japanese-owned car plant and a lot of call centres.'

No wonder football matters so much to this place. On one side of the stadium is a statue of manager Bob Stokoe running on to the pitch after that '73 Cup Final, his face an image of unalloyed joy beneath that battered hat. It's a reminder of the capacity of this game to lift the spirits of a community. Nearly 40 years on and the landscape of post-industrial Britain has left the people here even more dependent on Sunderland FC to give them a much-needed boost every now and then.

FAREWELL TO
ROKER PARK
1996/97
THE HEBBURN LADS

eah

RICAL SUPERSTORES
UNDERLAND ENTERPRISE PARK

 SUNDERLAND

SUNDERLAND VERSUS EVERTONT. THE HEBBURN LADS BID FAREWELL TO
ROKER PARK DURING SUNDERLAND'S LAST EVER MATCH, 3RD MAY 1997.

RON DAVIDSON'S PAINTING OF ROKER PARK.

SALTERGATE

Hatches were battened down. Windows were boarded up. Children were evacuated. Women fled to the hills or went back to their mothers . . . OK, I'm exaggerating slightly. It wasn't a full-scale Viking invasion; just the sort of preparations that a small English town felt obliged to make having drawn Glasgow Rangers in the long-defunct Anglo-Scottish Cup.

And so it came to pass that Chesterfield prepared to 'welcome' the Caledonian hordes on 28 October 1980, having already managed a very creditable 1–1 draw in the first leg at Ibrox. Some 500 police were deployed. The pubs closed down and most shops too. And that's not an exaggeration. 'There was a sandwich shop and the library open, and that was about it,' recalls Stuart Basson, author of Saltergate Sunset, the story of Chesterfield FC's venerable stadium. 'Their fans started turning up at eight in the morning and had nowhere to go.'

No wonder a scribe at the *Glasgow Herald* would later describe visiting Chesterfield as 'about as exciting as a night out with Ayatollah Khomeini'. As a technician at the local theatre, Stuart had to work that night and missed the game. But Andrew Jarvis, long-time football correspondent on the *Derbyshire Times*, was there and remembers a vibrant atmosphere created by nearly 14,000 fans, some 5,000 of them from Glasgow. He also remembers the result: 3–0 to Chesterfield with

two goals from Rangers reject Phil Bonnyman and another from Ernie Moss, a local lad who would become Chesterfield's all-time top scorer.

Andrew has spent half of his 52 years covering his beloved Spireites for the local paper, but he hadn't yet ascended into the press box on that eventful evening. He was just one of the crowd. 'I was living in Sheffield at the time and, after the game, we high-tailed it back to our local pub,' he confides. 'Suddenly a coach pulled up outside and out spilled all these Rangers fans. They were celebrating as though they'd won and seemed to think they were still in Chesterfield.'

So what happened next? 'They were boisterous but there was no trouble whatsoever.'

That seems to have been the pattern for the entire day. There were only six arrests and Saltergate's ancient fixtures and fittings survived.

11TH AUGUST 1939: THE TRAINER FOR CHESTERFIELD FOOTBALL CLUB, MR DAY SHOWS OFF THE NEW NUMBER ON THE
SHIRT OF THE CLUB'S CENTRE-FORWARD, MR MILLIGAN. IT WAS THE 1939/40 SEASON THAT PLAYERS FIRST WORE NUMBERS.

'My earliest impressions of Saltergate were that it was quite squalid. I used to go with my sister when we were small and, for big games against Mansfield Town or Notts County, we'd be manhandled down to the front of the terrace whether we wanted to go or not. The toilet facilities must have been practically non-existent because we had to wear wellies and it was obvious why. We were expected to watch the game practically ankle deep in urine.'

Even more surprisingly, perhaps, the ground is still standing today, although it hasn't hosted football since the last game was played here on 8 May 2010 – a 2–1 win over Bournemouth with a dramatic injury-time winner from Derek Niven, the club's longest serving player.

We're standing outside it now, Stuart, Andrew and I, gazing at the back of the old main stand, a grim vista of rusting corrugated iron. On the way here, I caught a glimpse of one of the floodlights towering over a row of bungalows. As with so many facilities – toilets, for instance – Saltergate acquired lights quite late in the day. Not until the 1967–68 season, indeed, which made Chesterfield the last League club in England to install them. 'It was our second attempt,' Stuart points out. 'The first floodlights were bought second hand from Sheffield United and, halfway through putting them up, they fell down again.'

It's fair to say that Chesterfield's long-term chairman Harold Shentall was not exactly Shirley Bassey material. But if he was no big spender, at least he was honest. The same could hardly be said of one of his more recent successors, Darren Brown, who finished up spending a spell as a guest of Her Majesty. The Serious Fraud Squad had been called into Saltergate in 2001. Brown eventually pleaded guilty to, among other things, filtering £800,000 out of the club for his own purposes. 'Prison finally catches up with Chesterfield's crooked Spireite' was one of the more memorable headlines at the time.

Enter the Chesterfield Football Supporters' Society, who heroically kept the fourth oldest club in the League going until printing company owner Barrie Hubbard took over as chairman in 2002. Saltergate had a lengthy tradition of self-help. Back in 1961, supporters helped raise the cash to raise a roof over the Kop end – or the Karen Child Kop as it was known after a Lottery winner put some of her winnings into the club.

We can see it now through a gap in the corrugated iron at the uncovered Cross Street end, where away supporters were accommodated from the 1970s onwards. Some of the turnstiles have been removed, much to Andrew's chagrin. 'It's like seeing a favourite aunt with her teeth out,' he confides.

It seems unlikely that the old girl will be around for too much longer. The ground has apparently been sold to Barratt Homes – 'for the

RELATIONS BETWEEN CHESTERFIELD AND MANSFIELD FANS DETERIORATED AFTER THE MINERS' STRIKE OF 1984–5. NORTH DERBYSHIRE MEMBERS WERE SOLIDLY BEHIND THE NATIONAL UNION OF MINEWORKERS; THEIR NEAR-NEIGHBOURS ACROSS THE NOTTINGHAMSHIRE BORDER FAR LESS SO. IN FACT, MANSFIELD BECAME THE HEADQUARTERS OF THE BREAKAWAY UNION OF DEMOCRATIC MINEWORKERS. NO WONDER THE HOME TERRACES AT SALTERGATE USED TO RESOUND TO CRIES OF 'SCABS' WHENEVER THE STAGS CAME TO TOWN AND CHESTERFIELD'S 5–2 VICTORY IN THE 1995 DIVISION THREE PLAY-OFF SEMI-FINAL WAS CELEBRATED WITH PARTICULAR RELISH.

SALTERGATE MADE IT ONTO THE BIG SCREEN IN 2009 WHEN IT WAS USED FOR LOCATION SCENES IN *THE DAMNED UNITED*, THE FILM OF DAVID PEACE'S MUCH DARKER NOVEL ABOUT BRIAN CLOUGH'S BROODING RIVALRY WITH DON REVIE. AN IDEAL LOCATION IT WAS, TOO. HAVING REMAINED IN A COBWEBBED TIME WARP, IT HAD ALL THE QUALITIES OF THE BASEBALL GROUND, DERBY, AS IT WAS IN THE EARLY 1970s.

second time', according to Stuart. 'Barratts bought it, on paper at least, towards the end of the Darren Brown era. But obviously that sale didn't go through.'

The need for a new ground had become a pressing issue in the 1990s when, in the wake of the Hillsborough disaster and the Bradford City fire, it became increasingly evident that Saltergate was not fit for purpose. A ground that had once hosted a crowd of 30,561 for a fifth-round cup tie against Tottenham in 1938 had been reduced in capacity to just 8,500, and this at a time when the club were enjoying some success on the field. In 1995 they beat their most keenly disliked rivals, Mansfield Town, 5–2 in a play-off semi-final before going on to win promotion to the third tier. And two years later they memorably reached the semi-final of the FA Cup, holding Middlesbrough to a 2–2 draw at Old Trafford before going down in the replay at Hillsborough. But it was the demand for tickets for the quarter-final against Nottingham Forest that once again emphasised Saltergate's shortcomings.

The new B2net Stadium can accommodate at least 2,000 more in comparatively palatial surroundings. It opened for business at the beginning of the 2010–11 season, largely thanks to the munificence of majority shareholder and former Sheffield Wednesday chairman Dave Allen. Unlike so many modern stadia, it's not on a bypass or some godforsaken retail park on the edge of town. It's a mile or two from Saltergate with a bus stop outside and a pub over the road. 'Supporters look back on the old place with fondness, but I don't get the feeling that too many of them would want to go back,' Stuart muses as we stand in the reception area surveying a surprisingly full trophy cabinet. The Johnstone's Paint Trophy was added in March 2012, shortly before the club was again relegated to the fourth tier.

And what's this other sizeable chunk of silverware? Of course! It's the Anglo-Scottish Cup. Chesterfield were the last winners back in 1980. 'I don't think anyone else knows where it is,' Stuart grins.

Rangers fans of a certain age probably do, though it seems unlikely that they'd be planning a return visit to Chesterfield any time soon.

THE LAST MATCH AT SALTERGATE. MAY 8, 2010 AGAINST BOURNEMOUTH.

SALTERGATE | 147

THE VETCH FIELD

From his house high up on steep streets, Gwyn Rees has a panoramic view of Swansea Bay, Mumbles and the Gower Peninsula. The only drawback in recent times has been that his eyes have felt morbidly drawn to a less pleasing sight a few hundred yards inland – the prolonged demolition of the Vetch Field, home of his beloved local football club from 1912 to 2005.

At least he has his memories, as well as files full of photos and old programmes lining the shelves of his study. In there somewhere will be documents pointing out that Swansea City were once called Swansea Town, that the ground was originally owned by the Swansea Gaslight Company and that the players had to wear kneepads for the first season because the surface was made up of compacted coal cinder spread over a field of vetch, used to feed cattle. Gwyn knows his stuff when it comes to the Swans. By day he's a postman, clambering up and down those steep streets without recourse to grappling hooks. But in his spare time he is the club's unofficial historian and it's all too evidently a labour of love.

Swansea made a lot of friends after becoming the first Welsh club to grace the Premier League at the beginning of the 2011–12 season. Not only did they accumulate more points in that season than anyone expected; their former manager Brendan Rodgers got them playing the game in the right way. All the more pleasing to see success at a club where the supporters' trust owns 20 per cent of the shares. The Swans nearly went out of business in 2001 when they were in the hands of an Australian-based businessman who had bought them for £1. They now have a new stadium and, remarkably, they're the only club in the Premier League with an elected supporter sitting on the board.

So when I ask Gwyn whether he misses the Vetch, it's not surprising that he hesitates for a moment before musing: 'I loved the place. It was where we grew up. I was 10 when I went to my first match there in 1964 against Crystal Palace. But let's not kid ourselves. It was a tip for the last few years. The toilet was just a wall to pee up. I don't know what women did, but I do know that we get a lot more young women coming to matches since we moved to the Liberty Stadium. The Vetch

1935 SWANSEA PLAYS WEST HAM

was a typical man's ground. I've got nothing against that, but there's no way we'd be where we are today if we'd stayed there.

'Good players wouldn't have wanted to come and we couldn't have got enough people in to watch. The capacity was down to 12,000 by the end to fit in with health and safety regulations. The North Bank was still terracing and they'd put up boards to make it smaller and reduce the chances of spectators being hurt. It was supposed to be a temporary measure, but it lasted about 12 years.'

Seven years have passed since the club moved to the Liberty, which sounds free and democratic but is, in fact, named after the sponsors, Liberty Property Holdings Ltd. That's modern football for you – just one element of a business plan that includes conference suites, Christmas party venues, rock concerts and, in this case, the Swans sharing their ground with Ospreys Rugby Club.

The Vetch, by contrast, was very much a relic of football's past. So what's going on there now? More than you might imagine, as we discover soon after Gwyn's VW Golf pulls up by the old turnstiles that are still standing at the junction of the Town End and the East Stand. Across the road is the prison. Any inmates who managed to position themselves by the bars in the upper reaches of the building on a Saturday afternoon must have had a grandstand view of the match. They might also have seen luxury coaches pulling up and disgorging some of the top players of the day. After all, Swansea have been in the top flight before. Back in the 1981–82 season they were briefly top of the First Division with a team that included Bob Latchford, Leighton James and Alan Curtis under the management of John Toshack.

'There's the players' entrance,' says Gwyn, pointing to a passageway between two modest end-of-terrace houses, one of which apparently belongs to Dolly Phillips, now 92, who used to make the teas and wash the kit. As if prearranged, two local residents appear with a key to the wrought-iron gates. 'Can we come in?' We can. And a surprisingly lively scene awaits us as we stroll down the passageway to the spot where the old dressing rooms used to be. It's a glorious spring evening and, up to the edge of the old pitch and beyond, there are allotments and stalls selling home-grown veg. Neighbours are sitting in garden chairs enjoying the final rays as the sun sinks behind one of the surrounding hills.

Mind you, this isn't any old community garden. This is 'Vetch Veg: an urban utopian growing revolution', according to one of the many posters hereabouts. 'It's part of a big public art work for the Welsh Cultural Olympiad,' explains community artist Owen Griffiths. 'The local community is being given chance to take ownership of the space while the council carry on trying to sell the land for housing.' Among the stalls is one displaying a pot of vetch, which looks like a blue-tinged herb. 'Is it edible?' 'Only if you're a cow,' I'm assured.

Beyond the stalls and allotments is a gravel path sweeping round a large circle of grass. In there somewhere we can just about make out the white line that marks the old centre circle. 'A lot of supporters'' ashes are under there,' Gwyn confides. 'They had to be relocated when we moved ground. Those that were in urns were dug up and given a proper Christian burial,' he adds as we head back to the car and set off to see his old mate Roy Griffiths.

Roy is a 75-year-old former welder who was nine when he saw his first match at the Vetch in 1946. 'Trevor Ford scored 40 goals for us that season, but it wasn't official because things were still settling down after the war and a lot of players were still stationed away from their home towns,' he recounts. 'Thursday was half-day closing and there'd usually be a match in the afternoon. No floodlights in those days. We'd come out of school at four and sneak in when they opened the gates with half an hour to go.'

Out come the photographs. Here's one of local boys Cliff Jones and Terry Medwin, who sped swiftly on the Swans' wings before flying off to the fabled Spurs Double-winning side of 1961. And here's one of Roy Paul, a former miner from the Rhondda who was part of the Swansea side that won the Third Division South title in 1948–49 before moving on to even greater glory with Manchester City. 'Roy Paul knew my father,' says Roy Griffiths. At his school in Swansea at the time, that was more important than your father having known Lloyd George.

After the photos come the memories. Of Ivor Allchurch, the 'Golden Boy of Welsh football' and 'nothing short of a genius', according to Roy. Gwyn concurs, having seen him at the end of his career when he returned to the Vetch after spells with Newcastle and 'them up the road'. Cardiff City in other words. Memories, too, of Harry 'the grafter' Griffiths, who would give great service to the club as a player and later as manager. Of watching Swansea beat Cardiff 5–1 in the 1949–50 season after climbing up the coal tip at the back of the North Bank. Roy recalls somebody at the back of the crowd saying: 'You'll never see a thing from there, boy.' So what did he do? 'He pushed me forward and the crowd parted like the Red Sea to let me down the front.'

Best of all, perhaps, was the game against Liverpool in 1959 or '60. 'My mate got married at ten o'clock that morning. We had the reception afterwards and it got to around one thirty or two o'clock. Things were breaking up a bit so I said: "Mervin, the Swans kick off at three. Ask your new missus if it's all right for us to go." She said yes as she had a few things to sort out at the flat they were moving into. So we shot down the ground in our best suits. We won 5–4 that afternoon.'

And the lucky old bridegroom still had his wedding night to come.

Reluctantly, it's time for me to bid farewell and catch a train to see 'them up the road'. I'm visiting Ninian Park, Cardiff, in the morning. As the train pulls out of Swansea, dusk has given way to nightfall, but the white-strutted exterior of the Liberty Stadium gleams like a little beacon in the darkness. It's a rum thought that exactly a century has passed since the players of what was then Swansea Town were donning kneepads to play on compacted coal cinder.

11TH MAY 2005. SWANSEA CITY V WREXHAM, FAW PREMIER CUP FINAL
FANS RIP THE VETCH APART COLLECTING SOUVENIRS AT THE END OF THE GAME

THE VICTORIA GROUND

It's a wet and murky mid-afternoon. The floodlights would have been on by now had this been a Saturday with Stoke City at home in the days when the great swathe of wasteland beyond that metal fence was their ground.

Peering through the railings and over chest-high weeds, it's difficult to believe that somewhere in this wilderness was once a football pitch graced by the likes of Gordon Banks and Peter Shilton, Jimmy Greenhoff and Mike Pejic, Alan Hudson and John Ritchie, Dennis Viollet, Jimmy McIlroy, Terry Conroy, Jackie Mudie, George Eastham and many more. Oh yes, and that chap Stan, born just down the road. Otherwise known as Sir Stanley Matthews, or 'the wizard of the dribble', the most iconic British footballer of the mid-20th century.

That century was drawing to a close on 4 May 1997, when Stoke beat West Bromwich Albion 2–1 in front of 22,500 fans to end their 119-year stay at the Victoria Ground. They reassembled after their holidays at the shiny new Britannia Stadium on the edge of town. For one reason or another, neither a giant Tesco nor an office development has materialised in the intervening 15 years. Did the property boom of the late 1990s and early 2000s pass Stoke by?

I'm still pondering why this should be when the steady deluge turns into an intense cloudburst and it seems prudent to climb back in the car.

'It's always like this in Stoke,' says Phil Dixon as the rain hammers down on the red roof of his otherwise black Mini. 'It'll stop in about three weeks.'

Phil, 60, used to be managing director of Smooth Radio, but he cut his teeth in the press box here, reporting on his beloved City for the *Newcastle-under-Lyme Times*. As in most press boxes before the advent of laptops and mobiles, there was usually a shortage of phones. 'The boys from the nationals were always trying to claim them for themselves and there'd be occasional scuffles,' he recalls.

Like his old school mate David Jenkins, who's wedged into the Mini's back seat, Phil witnessed a few scuffles on the terraces in over 35 years at the Victoria Ground, man and boy. David, who now reprints old *Wisden* cricket almanacs, was a long-haired student back home from North London Polytechnic and curious to see Law, Charlton and Best in the early 1970s when Manchester United played a home match at the Victoria Ground – this after their supporters' behaviour had managed to get them banned from Old Trafford for three games. Did it never occur

29TH APRIL 1965: SIR STANLEY MATTHEWS, AGED 50, PRESENTS A SOUVENIR BALL TO THE
SPECTATORS BEFORE PLAYING A FAREWELL MATCH FOR THE STANLEY MATTHEWS XI AGAINST A
WORLD XI AT STOKE CITY'S VICTORIA GROUND, WHERE HE BEGAN HIS CAREER 33 YEARS EARLIER.

THE BIGGEST CROWD EVER HOSTED AT THE VICTORIA GROUND WAS 51,380. THE VISITORS WERE ARSENAL AND THE DATE WAS 29 MARCH 1937. THE FOLLOWING SEASON STOKE FINISHED 17TH IN DIVISION ONE. DESPERATE TO WIN MEDALS, STANLEY MATTHEWS HANDED IN A TRANSFER REQUEST AND MORE THAN 3,000 SUPPORTERS ATTENDED A PROTEST MEETING WHILE ANOTHER 1,000 PARADED OUTSIDE THE GROUND WITH PLACARDS PLEADING WITH HIM NOT TO GO. STAN AGREED TO STAY FOR THE TIME BEING. THE SMALL MATTER OF THE SECOND WORLD WEAR INTERVENED BEFORE HE FINALLY SIGNED FOR BLACKPOOL FOR £11,500 IN 1947. ANOTHER SIX YEARS WOULD PASS BEFORE HE WON THAT MEDAL AND BLACKPOOL MEMORABLY LANDED THE FA CUP.

to the football authorities that the hooligan element would simply go and inflict themselves on other cities? Sure enough, there was a late surge at the uncovered Stoke End as kick-off approached and the incoming Reds turned the air around them blue. 'My dad was a primary school teacher and a bit of a martinet,' David explains. 'He turned round and bawled at them: "Would you people mind moderating your language." Me and my brother were mortified. Eventually the police escorted Dad from the ground for his own safety.'

Not surprisingly, David prefers to dwell on happier memories. One of the happiest goes all the way back to childhood. He was 12 and Phil was 11 in 1963 when Stoke marked their centenary by winning promotion to the First Division with a 2–0 victory over Luton Town. The fairytale was completed when Matthews latched on to a fine through ball from McIlroy and ran on to score. Along with thousands more, Phil duly dashed on the pitch from the Boothen End to celebrate. 'My shoes were caked with mud and I had a right telling off when I got home,' he recalls. Little did he know at the time that, on those few days when it hadn't been raining, Stoke had an arrangement with the local fire brigade to pop round and water the pitch before a home game. Matthews makes reference to the practice in his autobiography *Back in Touch*. A fire engine was dispatched to the Victoria Ground at crack of dawn every time City had a home game and the main beneficiary was

Stan himself. He was 48 at the time and troubled by an old knee injury that responded better to a softer, non-jarring surface.

The great man had rejoined Stoke from Blackpool two years previously. 'I was in the boys' enclosure for his first game back,' says Dave. 'It was against Huddersfield and some 35,000 tuned up. At the time we'd been drawing crowds of around 9,000.' Phil nods. 'They never allowed the team sheet to be published before a game because the gate would be down 15,000 if he wasn't playing. They waited until just before kick-off to make the announcement over the public address system. If his name was read out, there were huge cheers. If not, great groans and sighs swept around the ground.'

David was there for Matthews' final game against Fulham on 6 February 1965. Five days previously he had celebrated his 50th birthday. True to the script, he made one of City's goals as they went on to win 3–1 against a Fulham side that included Johnny Haynes, Bobby Robson and a youngster called Rodney Marsh. Matthews was up against left back Jim Langley, a spring chicken of 36. 'It was a typical Tony Waddington publicity coup,' David smiles. 'He didn't need to put Stan in the team. He hadn't played all season and we had a pretty good side in those days with the likes of Viollet, Dobing and McIlroy. But his inclusion ensured a bumper gate.'

'One of the games I'll never forget was against Ajax in September 1974. Stoke had qualified for the UEFA Cup by finishing fifth the previous season. You could say that I supported both teams but, although I was happy with the 1–1 draw, I really wanted Stoke to win. I'd been an admirer of the Dutch giants ever since they'd beaten Liverpool and I'd been over to Holland to watch them four or five times. Johan Cruyff had just left the club when they arrived in the Potteries. Still, they had players of the class of Ruud Krol. He scored with a 25-yard screamer after 30 minutes. But Denis Smith equalised with about 15 minutes to go. As I remember, he put everyone over the line from a corner and the ball with it. Stoke held them to a 0–0 draw in Amsterdam, but we went out on the away goals rule.'

Waddington was Stoke's manager from 1960 to 1977. Not only did he turn them into an established top-flight side; he also took them to two FA Cup semi-finals and landed the League Cup when they beat Chelsea in 1972. It was the only major trophy won by the second oldest club in the League after Notts County. Waddington it was who signed Gordon Banks from Leicester City in 1967, eventually replacing him with the only man fit to fill his boots when he paid Leicester a then-record fee for a goalkeeper. Peter Shilton took up residence between the Stoke sticks in 1974.

Two years later, however, fate intervened in the form of a howling gale. The roof blew off the Butler Street stand and the manager had to sell top players to help pay for the damage. Jimmy Greenhoff went to Manchester United, Alan Hudson to Arsenal and Waddington felt obliged to follow them out of the door the following year.

The Butler Street stand was on the opposite side of the wasteland from where we're parked, 10 yards or so from the entrance to the Boothen End and a Rory Delap throw-in from the uncovered Stoke End. Nearest to us would have been the main stand where Phil sat on the wooden benches of the press box, zealously protecting his phone. His formative years, though, were spent in the Boothen End where he once took the family's Christmas decorations. 'It was at a time when there was a craze for throwing toilet rolls from the terraces and watching them unfurl,' he explains. 'I just decided to throw a coloured streamer or two for a change. Everybody turned round to look.' As if to say, what's wrong with Bronco or Andrex? 'Something like that.' And didn't your parents notice they were missing? 'They did eventually and assumed that they must have been thrown out the previous Christmas.'

In those days Phil travelled in by bus from a village near Newcastle-under-Lyme, clutching his half-crown pocket money. Some of it went on the fare and one and six got him through the turnstiles. 'Stoke seemed like a Lowry painting in those days,' he muses. 'There were a lot of flat caps and mufflers about.'

It was even more of a culture shock for David, whose father had moved the family here from Oxford when he was nine. 'At least it's left me with some great football memories,' he suggests. 'I'm a season-ticket holder at the new ground, but I'm also a traditionalist and I love the idiosyncratic nature of old grounds like the Victoria.' Phil nods again. Then, with a regretful glance through the railings and across that rain-lashed wilderness, he starts the Mini.

It eventually comes to rest in the car park of the Britannia Stadium. On match days, some 28,000 fans (most of them local) generate a raucous

'My dad took me to the Victoria Ground for the first time when we were six. Until then I thought I was a Chelsea fan. In fact, we'd just signed Alan Hudson from Chelsea and Dad, who was not one for waxing lyrical, said after the game that he never gave the ball away once. The visitors that day were Leeds, who'd been unbeaten for 29 games. We duly went 2–0 down through goals from [Allan] Clarke and [Billy] Bremner after a very controversial free kick. But we came back strongly in the second half with goals from Mike Pejic and Hudson himself, Then Denis Smith got the winner with a diving header at the Boothen End and the place went wild. The Leeds fans didn't like it, of course, and I remember a copper's hat being thrown from the top to the bottom of the Stoke End. The Leeds players didn't like it either. Clarke was haranguing the referee all the way to the tunnel at the end of a game, which confirmed me as a lifelong Stoke fan.'

STOKE'S CHAIRMAN PETER COATES OWNS AN ONLINE BETTING COMPANY. BUT HE MADE HIS PILE FROM SOMETHING RATHER MORE ROOTED IN FOOTBALL FOLKLORE — PIES AND BOVRIL. WAGON WHEELS, TOO. HE SUPPLIED NOT JUST THE VICTORIA GROUND BUT FAMISHED FANS ALL OVER THE LAND. INDEED HE ONCE SOLD FAST FOOD TO ST MIRREN, WHERE THE MANAGER WAS RESPONSIBLE FOR JUST ABOUT EVERYTHING, INCLUDING ORDERING THE HALF-TIME PIES. HIS NAME WAS ALEC FERGUSON.

atmosphere. But on a wet Wednesday afternoon, the surroundings seem as soulless as any of the other business parks where so many new grounds are sited.

There are nods to the club's history here and there, notably a statue to Matthews on the edge of the Britannia's car park. Not so much the seven ages of man as the three ages of Stan – Stan the youth, Stan the man and Stan still with boot on ball in advanced middle age. Near the Delilah Bar and unfortunately close to a litter bin is a bust of John Ritchie, Stoke's all-time top scorer with 176 goals in 343 games.

Few were more memorable than the 'header' he scored against Southampton at a time when Waddington, having lured Alan Hudson away from Chelsea, was set on signing Peter Osgood as well. Osgood had other ideas. He signed for Southampton instead. David takes up

the tale: 'We played Southampton at the Victoria Ground in 1974 and Osgood made the mistake before the game of claiming that Ritchie was only any good with his head. Well, Stoke took them apart 4–1 and Ritchie bagged a hat-trick. For his final flourish, Ritchie rounded the goalkeeper, got down on his knees and nudged the ball over the line with his head.'

Sadly, Ritchie died in 2007. He was only 65 but suffering from complications arising from Alzheimer's disease, leading to speculation that footballers of his generation paid a price for heading too many of those heavy, wet case balls. Fans turned up for his funeral in some numbers. To a man and woman they will have remembered with gratitude the times when his goals illuminated the rickety old ground that their beloved club had said goodbye to almost 10 years previously. Memories that now lie buried under long grass and waste-high weeds on the wilderness that was once the Victoria Ground.

LEAGUE DIVISION ONE: STOKE CITY VERSUS WEST BROMWICH. SIR STANLEY MATTHEWS WAVES
FAREWELL AT THE VICTORIA GROUND AS STOKE CITY MOVE TO A NEW GROUND, 4TH MAY 1997.

THE VICTORIA GROUND | 159

BIBLIOGRAPHY

Camillin, Paul, and Weir, Stewart, *Albion: The First 100 Years*, Sports Pavilion, 2001

Carder, Tim, 'The Brighton Stadium Mystery' in Rebellion: The Growth of Football's Protest

Movement, edited by Dougie Brimson, John Blake, 2006

Foulger, Neville, *Farewell to Filbert Street*, Leicester City Publications, 2002

Grant, Len, *Full Time at Maine Road*, Len Grant Photography, 2004

Hornby, Nick, *Fever Pitch*, Gollancz, 1992; Penguin Modern Classics, 2012

Inglis, Simon, *The Football Grounds of England and Wales*, Willow Books, 1985

Watt, Tom, *The End: 80 Years of Life on Arsenal's North Bank*, Mainstream Publishing, 1993

INDEX